# A foundation for life

# a foundation for life

## A study of key Christian doctrines and their application

Michael A.G. Haykin, editor

*Contributors*
**David Aspinall, Pierre Constant, Heinz G. Dschankilic, Keith M. Edwards, Jim Elliff, David Kay, Stephen Kring, Jerry Marcellino, David B. Morris, Carl Muller, Peter Pikkert, Don Theobald, Kirk Wellum, Stephen J. Wellum, Fred G. Zaspel**

*press*

Dundas, Ontario

Joshua Press Inc., Dundas, Ontario, Canada
www.joshuapress.com

Editorial director: Michael A.G. Haykin
Creative/production manager: Janice Van Eck

© Cover & book design by Janice Van Eck

**National Library of Canada Cataloguing in Publication Data**

A foundation for life: a study of key Christian doctrines and their application /
  Michael A.G. Haykin, editor.

**ISBN 1-894400-17-8**

1. Theology, Doctrinal.  I. Haykin, Michael A.G.

BR121.2.F68 2002                    230                    C2002-901604-5

Dedicated with grateful thanks to Arend and Gerda Van Eck

# Contents

# Contributors

DAVID ASPINALL is Director of Apologia Home Mission to New Religions, a cult and apologetics ministry which he and his wife Vivian founded after leaving the Jehovah's Witnesses (the Watchtower) in 1987. The ministry library and office contains over 10,000 volumes on cults, controversial issues, as well as the Bible and theology. It is located in Mississauga, a suburb of Toronto, Canada. Apologia ministry (and book shop) may be contacted at dvapologia@look.ca.

PIERRE CONSTANT received a Ph.D. in New Testament Theology and Exegesis from Trinity International University, Deerfield, Illinois. He served in pastoral ministry for 15 years in Hull, Québec. He presently teaches at the École de Théologie Évangélique de Montréal. Pierre, his wife Lise, and their four children live in Aylmer, Québec.

HEINZ G. DSCHANKILIC is the Executive Director of Sola Scriptura Ministries International. He is a graduate of Central Baptist Seminary in Toronto. He has also served as the Managing Editor of *The Baptist Review of Theology* and serves as Marketing Consultant at Joshua Press, Dundas, Ontario. In addition, he is an adjunct faculty member of the William Carey School of Theology. Heinz is in a leadership position at Hespeler Baptist Church, Cambridge, Ontario. He is married to Cynthia (Wonnacott) and has two children, Lydia and Michael.

KEITH M. EDWARDS serves as a pastor of a rural, evangelical Baptist church in northeastern Ontario, the church in which he was raised. After growing up in a pastor's home, Keith studied at Central Baptist

Seminary in Toronto and served in administration and Christian Education in Toronto for 7 years before being called to pastor his home church. He is married to Ruth, a gifted musical director, and they have two daughters, Carolyn and Jane.

JIM ELLIFF is the president and founder of Christian Communicators Worldwide. Jim's conference speaking takes him around the world. Jim also has contributed to numerous books and periodicals and is the author of *Led by the Spirit: how the Holy Spirit guides the believer* (Joshua Press, 1999). His ministry is presented at www.CCWonline.org and www.WayToGod.org.

MICHAEL A.G. HAYKIN is currently Editorial Director of Joshua Press, Dundas, Ontario, and Professor of Church History at Heritage Theological Seminary in Cambridge, Ontario. He has a Th.D. in Church History from Wycliffe College and the University of Toronto (1982). He is the author of a number of books, including *One heart and one soul: John Sutcliff of Olney, his friends, and his times* (Evangelical Press, 1994) and *The armies of the Lamb: The spirituality of Andrew Fuller* (Joshua Press, 2001). He and his wife Alison have two children, Victoria and Nigel. They attend Trinity Baptist Church, Burlington, Ontario.

DAVID KAY has been the Pastor of Whiddon Valley Evangelical Church, a Reformed Baptist Church, in Barnstaple, North Devon, in the southwest of England for 8 years. He is married to Ruth and has four married children and six grandchildren. He trained at the London Reformed Baptist Seminary at the Metropolitan Tabernacle and has an MA from the University of the West of England, Bristol, U.K.

STEPHEN KRING was born in Pennsylvania, USA, where the Lord saved him at age five. He came to Toronto, Ontario in 1973 for theological training. Since his graduation from Toronto Baptist Seminary in 1977 with a B.Th., he has pastored Bethesda Baptist Church in Delhi, Ontario. He and his wife Cheryl have two sons and three daughters.

JERRY MARCELLINO has been a pastor since 1988 and has been the pastor of Audubon Drive Bible Church in Laurel, Mississippi, since 1993. Jerry is a graduate of the University of Hawaii—1980 (B.A.)—and Capital Bible Seminary in Lanham, Maryland—1988 (M.Div.). He is the author of *Rediscovering the Lost Treasure of Family Worship, Should Christians Have A Heart For Israel? A Biblical Perspective,* and *Should The Church Have A Heart for Israel? A Historical Perspective.* Jerry is presently serving as a member of the Executive Committee (Moderator *pro tem*) of *The Fellowship of Independent Reformed Evangelicals* (FIRE). He and his wife of 18 years, Dawn, are the parents of seven children.

DAVID B. MORRIS was converted in 1973 and entered an itinerant ministry of evangelism and conference speaking in September, 2001, after nearly twenty years in the pastorate. He studied Classics and Linguistics at the University of North Carolina at Chapel Hill. He and Terri, his wife of twenty years, have six children and live in Liverpool, Pennsylvania.

CARL MULLER is pastor of Trinity Baptist Church in Burlington, Ontario. He and his wife Heather have four children. Carl has been in the Christian ministry for over 20 years. He has a B.Th from Tyndale College, Toronto (1980) and a B.A. from the University of Waterloo, Ontario (1983).

PETER PIKKERT is a writer and teacher. He has a B.Th. from Prairie Bible Institute, a M.S.Sc. from Syracuse University and has studied at the universities of Jordan and Istanbul. He has worked for many years in the Middle East. He is the author of *Desecrated Lands, The Visitor, A Basic Course in Modern Kurmanji,* and *A Basic Course in Modern Turkish.* He has dual Dutch and Canadian citizenship, is married and has two children.

DON THEOBALD is pastor of Pilgrim Baptist Church, Ancaster, Ontario. He previously pastored Binbrook Baptist Church, Binbrook, Ontario, for 18 years. He has a B.Th. and a M.Div. from Tyndale College, Ontario, and a B.A. from the University of Waterloo, Ontario. He has also studied at Gordon-Conwell Seminary, Massachusetts. He is married to Marlene, and they have four grown children.

KIRK WELLUM is the founding and present pastor of Sovereign Grace Community Church in Sarnia, Ontario. He is married to Debbie, and they have been blessed with four children: Caleb, Brittany, Seth and Javan. Kirk received a B.Th from Tyndale College, Toronto, in 1980 and a B.A. from the University of Waterloo, Ontario, in 1982.

STEPHEN J. WELLUM is Associate Professor of Christian Theology at The Southern Baptist Theological Seminary, Louisville, Kentucky. He received his Ph.D. in Theological Studies (Systematic Theology major) from Trinity Evangelical Divinity School in 1996. He has published a number of articles in various journals such as *The Southern Baptist Theological Journal* and *Reformation and Revival Journal* and books such as *The Compromised Church: The Present Evangelical Crisis*, ed. John Armstrong (Wheaton: Crossway Books, 1998). From 1992 to 1996, he served as the Senior Pastor of Rose Hill Evangelical Free Church, Langford, South Dakota. He is married to Karen Ann and they have five children.

FRED G. ZASPEL is senior pastor of Cornerstone Church of Skippack, Pennsylvania, USA, following many years as senior pastor of Word of Life Baptist Church in Pottsville, Pennsylvania. He is also adjunct lecturer in New Testament at The Pennsylvania State University, Schuylkill Campus. He holds two M.A. degrees, a Th.M., and is currently a Ph.D. candidate. He presently lives just outside of Philadelphia, Pennsylvania, with his wife and their two children.

# Introduction

Absolutely central to Christianity is the fact that it involves a personal relationship with the one true, living God. This relationship begins in faith and trust: faith in the existence of God and trust in Jesus Christ—the perfect revelation of God and God himself—as one's Saviour and Lord. Like all good relationships that one treasures, it must be nurtured and developed. Nurturing this relationship, or what is sometimes called "growing in Christ," involves two important dimensions. First, there are spiritual disciplines that are vital, such things as prayer, reading and reflecting on the Bible, and fellowship with other Christians. And second, there is learning the Christian worldview and the fundamental beliefs Christians have held throughout the history of Christianity. The latter is sometimes called "Christian doctrine." Both of these dimensions of Christianity are utterly necessary to keeping the relationship with God alive and well.

The book you have in your hands is focused on the second of these dimensions, the doctrines that make up the Christian faith. It sets out as simply as possible what are the basic beliefs that Christians have held and gives support for them from the Bible.

The hope of the publishers is that this book will be a resource to new Christians to help orient them to what Christianity is all about and encourage them to study God's perfect revelation, the Bible. But we also hope that older Christian believers will benefit from this volume, reminding them of fundamental truths they need to cherish and think about.
—*Michael A.G. Haykin, editor*

God, in the gospel of His Son,
Makes His eternal counsels known;
Where love in all its glory shines,
And truth is drawn in fairest lines.

Here sinners of a humble frame
May taste His grace, and learn His name;
May read, in characters of blood,
The wisdom, power, and grace of God.

The prisoner here may break his chains;
The weary rest from all his pains;
The captive feel his bondage cease;
The mourner find the way of peace.

Here faith reveals to mortal eyes
A brighter world beyond the skies;
Here shines the light which guides our way
From earth to realms of endless day.

O grant us grace, Almighty Lord,
To read and mark Thy holy word;
Its truths with meekness to receive,
And by its holy precepts live.

*Benjamin Beddome (1717–1795) and*
*Thomas Cotterill (1779–1823)*

The doctrine of the Trinity and the doctrine of redemption, historically, stand or fall together. ...It is in this intimacy of relation between the doctrines of the Trinity and redemption that the ultimate reason lies why the Christian church could not rest until it had attained a definite and well-compacted doctrine of the Trinity. Nothing else could be accepted as an adequate foundation for the experience of the Christian salvation.

*B.B. Warfield (1851–1921)*

# 1 The Trinity

Fred G. Zaspel

If ever there was a distinctively Christian doctrine, it is the doctrine of the Trinity. It is one doctrine on which all Christians must agree. Yet this is, perhaps, the most difficult of all doctrines for us to grasp. "Trinity" means that God is both three and one. He is not three and one in the same way, of course; that would be nonsense. But God is one in being—there is only one true God—and yet he is three in persons—Father, Son and Spirit. These three persons are individual and distinct, but they share equally the same divine being. Each is God absolutely and without qualification, and ought not to be confused with the other. The Father is not the Son, nor is he the Spirit. The Son is neither the Father nor the Spirit. The Spirit is neither the Father nor the Son. Each is individual and distinct. Yet each is fully God, and all three together are the one and only God. Let us see how the Bible drives us to these conclusions.

## The oneness of God

The most basic truth about our God is that he is one. He is not many, and he is not one among many. He is God alone. God is not "they" or "them" but "he" and "him." He is

**Deuteronomy 4:39**
"Therefore know this day, and consider it in your heart, that the LORD Himself is God in heaven above and on the earth beneath; there is no other."

**Deuteronomy 6:4**
"Hear, O Israel: The LORD our God, the LORD is one!"

**Deuteronomy 32:39a**
'Now see that I, even I am He, And there is no God besides Me.'

**Isaiah 44:6–8**
"Thus says the LORD, the King of Israel, And his Redeemer, the LORD of hosts: 'I am the First and I am the Last; Besides Me there is no God. And who can proclaim as I do? Then let him declare it and set it in order for Me, Since I appointed the ancient people. And the things that are coming and shall come, Let them show these to them. Do not fear, nor be afraid; Have I not told you from that time, and declared it? You are My witnesses. Is there a God besides Me? Indeed there is no other Rock; I know not one.'"

**1 Corinthians 8:5–6**
For even if there are so-called gods, whether in heaven or on earth (as there are many gods and many lords), yet for us there is one God, the Father, of whom are all things, and we for Him; and one Lord Jesus Christ, through whom are all things, and through whom we live.

**1 Timothy 2:5**
For there is one God and one Mediator between God and men, the Man Christ Jesus.

one. We call this God's *unity* and refer to this doctrine as *monotheism*. God is "the only true God" (John 17:3), and "God is one" (Galatians 3:20).

The Bible insists that our God is one and that he is the only one. This is a heavy concern throughout the Scriptures, and it is the basis of God's claim to our exclusive loyalty, love and worship (Deuteronomy 4:35,39; 6:4; 32:39a; 1 Kings 8:60; Isaiah 44:6–8; 45:5–6,21–22; Romans 3:30; 1 Corinthians 8:5–6; Galatians 3:20; 1 Timothy 2:5; James 2:19).

### The Old Testament: the plurality of God

What sometimes is puzzling is the fact that the Scriptures often refer to God in plural terms. For example, one of the Hebrew words for "God" is *elohim*, and it is a word used hundreds of times over throughout the Old Testament. What is interesting is that the word is plural in form and would ordinarily be translated "gods," yet the verbs that are used with this noun are regularly in the singular.

For instance, Genesis 1:1, translated very literally, reads "In the beginning Gods (he) created the heavens and the earth." There is unity—"he created," but there is plurality in the word "God."

Similarly, in Genesis 1:26 we read, "Then God said, 'Let Us make man in Our image, according to Our likeness.'" Again the word "God" is plural, and the verb ("he said") is singular. Even the pronouns speak in plural terms—"us," "our"; moreover, notice that it is "our" (plural) and "image" (singular).

These kinds of statements are found throughout the Old Testament, confirming clearly that in some sense God is a unity and at the same time a plurality (Genesis 3:22; 11:6–7; Isaiah 6:8).

In the same way the Old Testament often presents "the angel of the Lord" both as one who is *sent from* God, and so distinct from him, and as one who is himself God, and so one with God (Exodus 23:20–21; Judges 6:11–24; 13:2–23).

Similarly, there are many "Spirit of God" passages throughout the Old Testament in which the Spirit, who is God, is yet distinct from God (Genesis 1:2; Isaiah 61:1; 63:7–10).

Furthermore, there are many places in the Old Testament where two are referred to or even addressed as God. Indeed, sometimes God himself addresses God as one distinct from himself (Psalm 45:6–7; 110:1; Hosea 1:7).

The evidence goes still further. Isaiah is a prophet noted for his insistence on monotheism (Isaiah 44:6–8; 45:5–6,21–22). Yet in Isaiah 48:16 the inspired prophet identifies *three* divine persons (see also verses 12–15; compare Isaiah 61:1).

In Isaiah 48, God himself speaks. Yet he speaks of himself as sent from God and from the Spirit of God. There is the God who sends, the Spirit of God who sends, and the God who is sent. This God who is one is spoken of as three in persons.

In some sense, therefore, God is both one and a plurality. All this clearly anticipates a fuller revelation, a more complete explanation.

**Isaiah 6:8**
Also I heard the voice of the Lord, saying: "Whom shall I send, And who will go for Us?" Then I said, "Here *am* I! Send me."

**Psalm 45:6–7**
Your throne, O God, *is* forever and ever; A scepter of righteousness is the scepter of Your kingdom. You love righteousness and hate wickedness; Therefore God, Your God, has anointed You With the oil of gladness more than Your companions.

**Psalm 110:1**
The LORD said to my Lord, "Sit at My right hand, Till I make Your enemies Your footstool."

**Hosea 1:7a**
"Yet I will have mercy on the house of Judah, Will save them by the Lord their God."

**Isaiah 48:16**
"Come near to Me, hear this: I have not spoken in secret from the beginning; From the time that it was, I *was* there. And now the LORD GOD and His Spirit Have sent Me."

But already it is clear that God is one, yet there are a plurality of persons who are God.

### The New Testament: the three persons who are God

It is the New Testament writers who most clearly present this God of unity-in-plurality. Here we are taught explicitly both that God is one and that there are three persons who are God. Each of these three persons is God, yet they each are separate, or distinct, persons. Our God is Father, Son and Holy Spirit—or, to use the Apostle Paul's vocabulary, he is God, the Lord Jesus Christ and the Holy Spirit.

First, there is God the Father. That he is God, no one questions. Jesus identifies our "heavenly Father" as God in Matthew 6:26–30 (see also John 6:27; John 17:1–3). The Apostle Paul speaks similarly in his common reference to "God our Father" (Romans 1:7; 1 Corinthians 8:6; Galatians 1:1). There is therefore, the Father who is God.

There is also the Son who is God. He is "the Mighty God" whose coming is promised (Isaiah 9:6). He is born in Bethlehem and yet comes from eternity (Micah 5:2). His name is "God with us" (Isaiah 7:14; Matthew 1:23). He is God from eternity (John 1:1), "our great God and Saviour" (Titus 2:13), "the true God" (1 John 5:20) and "the eternally blessed God" (Romans 9:5). He is Man, to be sure—this is the mystery of the incarnation. Christ is God come in the flesh (John 1:14)! "For in Him dwells all the fullness of the Godhead bodily"

**John 17:3**
"And this is eternal life, that they may know You, the only true God, and Jesus Christ whom You have sent."

**Romans 1:7**
To all who are in Rome, beloved of God, called *to be* saints: Grace to you and peace from God our Father and the Lord Jesus Christ.

**Galatians 1:1**
Paul, an apostle (not from men nor through man, but through Jesus Christ and God the Father who raised Him from the dead).

**Micah 5:2**
"But you, Bethlehem Ephrathah, *Though* you are little among the thousands of Judah, *Yet* out of you shall come forth to Me The One to be Ruler in Israel, Whose goings forth *are* from of old, From everlasting."

(Colossians 2:9). He is *both* the Son of David *and* the Son of God (Matthew 22:41–46). Few today would question Christ's humanity, but Scripture affirms both that he is God and that he is man.

Although he is God, he is not the Father. They are two distinct persons. On the cross he was forsaken of God (Matthew 27:46). He was sent from the Father (John 3:16) and came to do the Father's will (John 6:38); and he is bruised by the Father (Isaiah 53:10). He is the Father's Son (Psalm 2:7).

There is, then, God the Father, and there is God the Son. Both are God—the same God! Yet they are not the same persons. They are distinct as to their personalities and yet united in a single deity.

Finally, there is the Spirit who is God. He is commonly called "the Spirit of God," the Spirit of the Lord" and "the Spirit of the Lord God." Believers in Christ are "God's temple" (1 Corinthians 3:16) precisely because the Holy Spirit indwells them. The Bible is inspired of *God* (2 Timothy 3:16) because it was God the Holy Spirit who superintended and carried along the biblical writers in their work (2 Samuel 23:2; 2 Peter 1:21). And in Acts 5, Ananias' lie to the Holy Spirit was a lie to God (see verses 3–4).

But again, although the Holy Spirit is God, he is not to be identified with the Father or the Son. They are distinct. He is "another Helper" (John 14:16)—another helper like Jesus, yes, but "another" helper, not the same. He is sent by the Lord Jesus (John

**Matthew 27:46**
And about the ninth hour Jesus cried out with a loud voice, saying, "Eli, Eli, lama sabachthani?" that is, *"My God, My God, why have You forsaken Me?"*

**John 6:38**
"For I have come down from heaven, not to do My own will, but the will of Him who sent Me."

**1 Corinthians 3:16**
Do you not know that you are the temple of God and *that* the Spirit of God dwells in you?

**2 Peter 1:21**
...for prophecy never came by the will of man, but holy men of God spoke *as they were moved* by the Holy Spirit.

**John 14:16**
"And I will pray the Father, and He will give you another Helper, that He may abide with you forever."

**John 15:26**
"But when the Helper comes, whom I shall send to you from the Father, the Spirit of truth who proceeds from the Father, He will testify of Me."

**Romans 8:27**
Now He who searches the hearts knows what the mind of the Spirit *is*, because He makes intercession for the saints according to *the will* of God.

**Matthew 28:19**
"Go therefore and make disciples of all the nations, baptizing them in the name of the Father and of the Son and of the Holy Spirit."

**1 Corinthians 12:4–6**
There are diversities of gifts, but the same Spirit. There are differences of ministries, but the same Lord. And there are diversities of activities, but it is the same God who works all in all.

15:26; 16:7) and by the Father (John 14:26), and he makes intercession with the Father for us in prayer (Romans 8:27).

These three are God—the one and only God. Yet they are three. We must understand that they are not one *in the same sense* that they are three. They are one in essence yet three in persons—three distinct persons in the one God. There is plurality and unity in the Godhead. God is a unity, yes. But he is also a plurality. He is a tri-unity.

This is reflected in "the great commission" in Matthew 28:19. Notice it is a single "name." Yet there are three who share the name of God. This name of God is now known as the Father, the Son, and the Holy Spirit. Three distinct individuals are specified, but they share equally the one name of God.

### New Testament allusions to the Trinity
Interestingly, the tri-unity of God is not *taught* in the New Testament as much as it is *presumed*. As we read the New Testament we find that God as three in one is a matter of common belief in the early Christian church. It is a belief already held and assumed by those to whom the apostles write.

For example, in 1 Corinthians 12:4–6 Paul speaks freely and without further explanation of the Trinitarian source of spiritual gifts. Our spiritual gifts come from "the Spirit" and from "the Lord" (Jesus), and from "God" (the Father). Similarly, in 2 Corinthians 13:14 the Apostle traces our redemptive blessings to each, the Lord Jesus Christ, God the

Father and the Holy Spirit. Our salvation stems from the elective purpose of God the Father (Ephesians 1:3–6), is grounded in the redemptive work of the Son (Ephesians 1:7–13) and is applied to us and kept for us by the Holy Spirit (Ephesians 1:13–14; see also Ephesians 4:4–6; 1 Peter 1:2; Jude 20–21).

These allusions to the Trinity, found throughout the New Testament, reveal that this was a faith shared by all Christians in the early church. It was not an article of faith that demanded proof or defense.

## The Trinity and the gospel

It is common to read in books of theology that the doctrine of the Trinity is *revealed* theology. It is not something we have figured out by ourselves; it is something God has revealed about himself. Nor is it a matter of what we call general revelation; it is not something we can learn from the created order around us. It is a matter of *special* revelation. If God had not told us this in his Word, we never could have learned it at all. We know nothing of God's tri-unity apart from special revelation, and we can know nothing *more* of it than he has told us. This is revealed theology in every sense of the term.

But it is interesting to learn *how* and *when* God revealed this about himself. We have noted how God's plurality in unity was alluded to throughout the Old Testament Scriptures. We have noted also that this doctrine is reflected in the New Testament writings as an already-held, universally

Ephesians 1:10–14
...that in the dispensation of the fullness of the times He might gather together in one all things in Christ, both which are in heaven and which are on earth—in Him. In Him also we have obtained an inheritance, being predestined according to the purpose of Him who works all things according to the counsel of His will, that we who first trusted in Christ should be to the praise of His glory. In Him you also *trusted*, after you heard the word of truth, the gospel of your salvation; in whom also, having believed, you were sealed with the Holy Spirit of promise, who is the guarantee of our inheritance until the redemption of the purchased possession, to the praise of His glory.

1 Peter 1:2
...elect according to the foreknowledge of God the Father, in sanctification of the Spirit, for obedience and sprinkling of the blood of Jesus Christ: Grace to you and peace be multiplied.

Jude 20–21
But you, beloved, building yourselves up on your most holy faith, praying in the Holy Spirit, keep yourselves in the love of God, looking for the mercy of our Lord Jesus Christ unto eternal life.

believed truth among those Christians to whom the apostles wrote. The apostles do not *argue* the fact so much as they *assume* it of their readers. How do we account for this? How is it that the strict monotheism held by them as Jews (Luke is the only non-Jewish writer in Scripture) suddenly became a Trinitarian monotheism?

The answer, it seems, is that the New Testament was written by and to those Christians who *witnessed* the revelation of the Trinity first-hand. They had seen with their own eyes that God had sent his Son into the world and that the Son had revealed him. They had witnessed the baptism of Jesus and had heard the voice from heaven and had seen the Spirit descending in the form of a dove. They had witnessed the descent of the Spirit at Pentecost and had experienced his revelation of the triune God to them. They had seen in Christ the revelation of the triune God and had come to experience his presence by means of the Spirit. God's tri-unity, in other words, was revealed in fact and in deed before it was revealed in word.

That is to say, God revealed himself as triune only as he revealed himself in the gospel. He has shown himself to be three in one only in the outworking of his saving purpose. This, God's highest self-revelation, is a gospel revelation. God promised to save, and in the outworking of that promise he revealed himself as Father, Son and Spirit. The Father sent the Son to accomplish the saving mission. The Father and the Son sent the Spirit to apply his saving work to his people and to mediate the presence of God to them. The Trinity is a gospel revelation, and it is a gospel-centered revelation.

## The Trinity and Christian worship

Finally, how should this affect us as believers? In a word, our knowledge of this great truth should make us better worshippers. We have a three-person God who has become for us all that we could ever need. He has chosen us in grace. He has come for us and has taken upon himself the penalty of our sin against him. And he has come to dwell in us and to make us his own. In light of all this, then, we should cultivate a more Trinitarian worship. It is through Christ, God the Son, and it is by the Holy Spirit, that we enter the Father's presence. It is the Three whom we worship, not the Father only. When we pray, it is to the Father, in the name of the Son, and by the help of the Spirit. We praise him—Father, Son and Spirit—for his gracious work on our behalf and in us. In short, we must learn to live every day of our lives finding comfort, strength and encouragement in "the grace of the Lord Jesus Christ, and the love of God, and the communion of the Holy Spirit" (2 Corinthians 13:14).

What does creation show about God? Primarily it shows his great power and wisdom, far above anything that could be imagined by any creature. "It is he who made the earth by his power, who established the world by his wisdom, and by his understanding stretched out the heavens" (Jeremiah 10:12). In contrast to ignorant men and the "worthless" idols they make, Jeremiah says, "Not like these is he who is the portion of Jacob, for he is the one who formed all things...the LORD of hosts is his name" (Jeremiah 10:16). One glance at the sun or the stars convinces us of God's infinite power. And even a briefer inspection of any leaf on a tree, or of the wonder of the human hand, or of any one living cell, convinces us of God's great wisdom. Who could make all of this? Who could make it out of nothing? Who could sustain it day after day for endless years? Such infinite power, such intricate skill, is completely beyond our comprehension. When we meditate on it, we give glory to God.

*Wayne Grudem (1948– )*

# 2 God the Creator

Stephen J. Wellum

It is hard to overestimate the importance of the doctrine of creation. In Scripture, God first identifies himself as the sovereign Creator and thus the Lord of his universe. Many Christians are naturally interested in the doctrine of salvation, but without the God of creation and providence, there is no Christianity as the Bible describes it. Indeed, the theological underpinnings for the doctrine of salvation are rooted in the fact that the God who is there, the sovereign, personal, triune Lord who has existed from all eternity, at a moment, spoke this universe into existence out of nothing. And as such, everything and everyone is utterly dependent upon him and responsible to him.

The doctrine of creation, along with providence, should be viewed as the outworking and execution of God's eternal plan or decree. Scripture is clear that the decree of God is his eternal plan by which, before the creation of the world, he purposed to bring to pass everything that happens (Psalm 139:16; Proverbs 16:4; 19:21; Isaiah 14:24–27; 37:26; 46:10–11; Acts 2:23; 4:27–28; 17:26; Romans 8:28–29; 9:1–33; Galatians 4:4–5; Ephesians 1:4,11–12; 2:10). Creation is the outworking of that eternal plan with respect to the origin

**Psalm 139:16**
Your eyes saw my substance, being yet unformed. And in Your book they all were written, the days fashioned for me, when *as yet there were* none of them.

**Isaiah 14:24–27**
The LORD of hosts has sworn, saying, "Surely, as I have thought, so it shall come to pass, And as I have purposed, *so* it shall stand...This *is* the purpose that is purposed against the whole earth, And this *is* the hand that is stretched out over all the nations. For the LORD of hosts has purposed, And who will annul *it*? His hand *is* stretched out, And who will turn it back?"

**Romans 8:28–29**
And we know that all things work together for good to those who love God, to those who are the called according to *His* purpose. For whom He foreknew, He also predestined *to be* conformed to the image of His Son, that He might be the first-born among many brethren.

of the universe and all that exists, including angelic and human beings. Providence, on the other hand, is the outworking of God's eternal plan in time and in relationship to the world he has made in terms of his preserving and governing all things to their appointed ends for his own glory (Psalm 103:19; 136:25; 145:15; Daniel 4:34–35; Acts 17:28a; Romans 11:36; Ephesians 1:11; Colossians 1:17; Hebrews 1:3). God, in identifying himself as the sovereign God of creation and providence, makes it very clear that he alone is God and there is none else, that he will share his glory with no created thing, and that he deserves all of our worship, praise and obedience (Isaiah 40–48; Jeremiah 10:1–16; John 17:3; 1 Timothy 1:17).

### The meaning of the doctrine of creation

When we affirm that God is the creator is there anything more specific that we can say? In other words, what exactly are we affirming and thus also denying? Let us first start with what we are affirming before we turn our attention to what we are denying. The meaning of the Christian doctrine of creation may be stated in at least three truths.

First, God created the universe out of nothing. Scripture begins by affirming that "in the beginning God created the heavens and the earth" (Genesis 1:1). Before God began to create the universe, nothing existed except the triune God himself. However at a moment, the eternal God spoke and brought this space-time universe into existence "out of nothing," that is, without the use of any previously existing materials. It is because of this fact that Scripture and Christian theology affirms that matter is not eternal, but a created reality. In other words, God alone is the self-existing God and everything else is dependent upon him:

**Genesis 1:1**
In the beginning God created the heavens and the earth.

- God is the Creator of all things (Genesis 1:1; Psalm 33:6,9; 96:5; Isaiah 40:28; John 1:3; Acts 4:24; 14:15; 17:24–25; Ephesians 3:9; Colossians 1:16; Revelation 4:11).
- God created all things "out of nothing" (Genesis 1:1; Psalm 33:9; Romans 4:17; Hebrews 11:3).

**Colossians 1:16**
For by Him all things were created that are in heaven and that are on earth, visible and invisible, whether thrones or dominions or principalities or powers. All things were created through Him and for Him.

Second, God created the universe freely. Scripture nowhere presents God as needing to create out of some kind of necessity either outside of him or internal to him. Rather, he, as the triune God, is self-existent and self-sufficient, and freely decides to create. In this important sense, God did not have to create a universe. Rather, owing to his own sovereign choice and for his own good pleasure, he purposed to create. That is why Scripture affirms that God does not need the world, but that the world and all that is in it is utterly and completely dependent upon him (Isaiah 43:7; 46:5–13; Jeremiah 10:12–16; Job 12:10; Acts 17:25,28; Revelation 4:11).

**Hebrews 11:3**
By faith we understand that the worlds were framed by the word of God, so that the things which are seen were not made of things which are visible.

**Isaiah 43:7**
"Everyone who is called by My name, Whom I have created for My glory; I have formed him, yes, I have made him."

Third, creation is an act of the triune God. Creation is not only the work of the Father, it is also the work of the Son, and the activity of the Spirit:

- the work of the Father in creation (Genesis 1:1; Psalm 19:1–2; 33:6,9; 96:5; 136:5–9; Isaiah 40:28; Jeremiah 10:12; Acts 17:24–25; Ephesians 3:9; Revelation 4:11)
- the work of God the Son in creation (John 1:1–3; 1 Corinthians 8:6; Colossians 1:15–17; Hebrews 1:2)
- the work of God the Spirit in creation (Genesis 1:2; Job 33:4; Psalm 104:30)

As an act of the triune God, the reason the world was created is ultimately for God's own glory.

Just as important as it is to state what we mean positively about the doctrine of creation, it is also necessary to stress what we do not mean by it. The Bible's view of creation stands over against both ancient and contemporary views of origins. In particular, the Bible rejects the following false views regarding the origins of the universe and of human beings.

First, Scripture rejects all naturalistic and evolutionary views of origins. Naturalism, at its heart, attempts to view origins solely in light of naturalistic processes involving the evolution of matter by chance over a period of time. It is through this explanation that people attempt to explain all of the complexity and order of the universe, including human beings. In this view, matter is viewed as eternal or at least self-generating, independent of the sovereign will of God. Scripture rejects this view outright.

Second, Scripture rejects all pantheistic views of origins. In this view, there is no ultimate distinction made between the Creator and the creation; God and the world are essentially one. And furthermore, the world is often explained as a necessary emanation or outflow of the whole of reality—the One. Scripture makes it very clear that the eternal, transcendent God will not be reduced to his created order, and that fundamental to a Christian view of the world is the Creator-creature distinction that pantheism denies.

Third, Scripture rejects all dualistic understandings of the universe. In dualism, there are two distinct co-eternal substances or principles from which all else is derived. Dualism often views these two principles as two antagonistic spirits—good and evil. Once again, Scripture is clear that God alone is God, that he has no rivals, and that he will share his glory with no one.

What these three false views have in common is that they attempt to deny the glorious God of creation. The Apostle Paul reflects upon this sad situation in Romans 1:18–32, arguing that the existence of the God of creation is clearly known to all people, but owing to the rebelliousness of the human heart, the truth of God has been willfully suppressed and distorted by us. Instead of glorifying the God who has made us and giving him thanks, we have exchanged the glory of God for created realities. The end result, rightly and sadly, is the just, righteous and holy wrath of God being brought upon us because of our sin and depravity. The only hope for us, in such a situation, is the sovereignty of God in grace and redemption.

**Romans 1:18–24**
For the wrath of God is revealed from heaven against all ungodliness and unrighteousness of men, who suppress the truth in unrighteousness, because what may be known of God is manifest in them, for God has shown it to them. For since the creation of the world His invisible attributes are clearly seen, being understood by the things that are made, even His eternal power and Godhead, so that they are without excuse, because, although they knew God, they did not glorify Him as God, nor were thankful, but became futile in their thoughts, and their foolish hearts were darkened. Professing to be wise, they became fools, and changed the glory of the incorruptible God into an image made like corruptible man—and birds and four-footed animals and creeping things. Therefore God also gave them up to uncleanness, in the lusts of their hearts, to dishonor their bodies among themselves, who exchanged the truth of God for the lie, and worshiped and served the creature rather than the Creator, who is blessed forever. Amen.

### The theological and practical significance of the doctrine of creation

What is the theological and practical significance of the doctrine of creation? There are many points that could be made, but at least three reflections are in order.

1) The doctrine of creation identifies for us our glorious God.

   Creation reminds us that the God who made it is no small, insignificant deity. No, he is the Lord over all, the source of all that there is, and the one who alone is sovereign. Furthermore, creation reminds us that he is not a far-off deity. Rather, he is the "covenant Lord," the one who is the living and active God, intimately involved in and with his creation, continually upholding, sustaining and governing his creation, and entering into covenant relationship with his people. Indeed, our God is truly great, full of majesty and glory, wisdom, strength and power because he is God the Creator.

2) The doctrine of creation tells us something about ourselves as God's creatures.

   It is precisely because we are God's creatures, created in his image, that human beings enjoy a unique role in creation. Ironically, when people attempt to live apart from God and deny their Creator in both their lives and thought, they find that they cannot understand themselves correctly. Thus, they end up viewing themselves as less than they are, say as grown-up animals or human machines, who have little significance and value. But the Christian view of human beings, tied to the doctrine of creation, tell us that God made us with dignity and value and that this, at the end of the day, is the only basis for a proper understanding of human beings. Furthermore, the fact of our creation by God also serves as the foundation for all ethics, human responsibility and a correct understanding of our place in this world as stewards, under God, of his creation. But once again, because of our willful rejection of our Creator and Lord, we have set ourselves against him, and thus stand in need of redemption, a redemption that only God can sovereignly bring about and accomplish.

3) The doctrine of creation tells us something about our world in two important areas.

The first area has to do with how we should view this world in terms of value. Because God created this world, it is important to stress that it has value. This is made evident in Genesis 1 by God's value judgment of "It was good" (Genesis 1:4,10,12,18,21,25) and his summary evaluation "It was very good" (Genesis 1:31). In this context, "good" indicates that it was not only what God had purposed and intended but also that the world has incredible worth. God said "Yes!" to what he had made. An important implication of this for Christian theology is not to elevate both in our thinking and practice, the "spiritual" over the "physical." This has been a problem in the

**Genesis 1:31**
Then God saw everything that He had made, and indeed *it was* very good. So the evening and the morning were the sixth day.

past and has produced various misunderstandings in the church. God, in creating this world, values both physical and spiritual reality. Sadly, as a result of the Fall, both are now cursed. But in redemption, God has done a work in Christ that not only saves the soul but also the body. Hence, the emphasis in Scripture on the resurrection of our bodies to live in a new heavens and a new earth in the presence of God forever (1 Corinthians 15; Revelation 21–22).

The second area has to do with the Christian understanding of God's ongoing relation to and involvement with his universe and its implications for a Christian view of science. Of course, much could be said on this point. Suffice it to say that since the created order is the result of the free choice of the personal, sovereign Lord, it too is designed, ordered, structured and law-governed. But, in its structure, the creation is never to be viewed merely in mechanistic terms. Christian theology rejects any notion of either an "open" or "closed" universe.

An "open" universe is the view represented by animism. Animism does not view the universe as being under the sovereign control of God but, instead, as controlled by fickle spirits and forces.

A "closed" universe view is the view represented by modern science. In this latter view, the universe is conceived as solely under the control of mechanistic laws independent of the will and plans of God, and thus this view conceives of the miraculous as impossible.

Scripture, however, rejects both of these views. Instead, Scripture presents us with a "controlled" universe. The scriptural view sees this world as orderly and predictable owing to its relation to the God of creation and providence. But it also affirms that this world is not independent of God, and that if God so chooses, he may act in this world and bring about his plans and purposes in extraordinary and miraculous ways. Thus, the Christian view of the world, tied to our doctrine of creation, allows us to view the world in a predictable, orderly fashion and thus allows for science. While at the same time, the concept of miracles is not a problem given the fact that the God of creation is also the God of providence who continually sustains and, if he so chooses, acts in the world.

From this brief overview, it is not hard to see that the doctrine of creation and the affirmation that God is the Creator are of critical importance for Christian theology. As already stated, without the God of creation and providence, there is no Christianity as the Bible describes it. All other doctrines, including the doctrine of salvation, are rooted and grounded in the fact that God is the sovereign creator and Lord of his universe. For the God who acts in sovereign power in creation is also the God who acts in sovereign grace in redemption. Indeed, the doctrine of creation is also foundational to Christian theology in another sense—it is the beginning of the story that leads to redemption. In insisting on the goodness of God's initial creation, the Bible sets the stage for what goes wrong—sin, death, destruction and the development of the story line of Scripture that issues in a Redeemer to set it right. Ultimately, the whole drama of redemptive history anticipates the restoration of goodness, even the transformation to a greater glory, of the universe gone wrong (Romans 8:18–27), and arrives finally at the dawning of a new heaven and a new earth (Revelation 21–22), the home of righteousness (2 Peter 3:13).

**2 Peter 3:13**
Nevertheless we, according to His promise, look for new heavens and a new earth in which righteousness dwells.

One thing at least is clear: even if the belief in the virgin birth is not necessary to every Christian, it is necessary to Christianity...Let it never be forgotten that the virgin birth is an integral part of the New Testament witness about Christ, and that that witness is strongest when it is taken as it stands. Only one Jesus is presented in the Word of God; and that Jesus did not come into the world by ordinary generation, but was conceived in the womb of the virgin by the Holy Ghost.

*J. Gresham Machen (1881–1937)*

# 3 The virgin birth

Heinz G. Dschankilic

As a number of Christian authors have observed in the past, the virgin birth is actually a virgin conception. The central issue revolves around the way in which Jesus Christ was conceived in the womb of Mary. Over the past two thousand years, biblical Christianity has affirmed both the historical reality of Christ's birth from a woman who was sexually a virgin at the time of her conception and that this conception was miraculously effected by the Holy Spirit.

## The virgin birth—an historical reality

Our affirmation of the virgin birth is rooted in the accounts provided in Matthew 1:18–25 and Luke 1:26–38.

In the account in Matthew we are told the following:

- Mary is called his mother (1:18; 2:13). Joseph is not, in these texts, called his father.
- Mary (1:19) is pregnant and the cause of her pregnancy is stated in the negative— "before they came together"—and in the positive—"through the Holy Spirit." Any human factor is clearly ruled out. Divine agency is clearly highlighted.
- Joseph (1:19) is certain of his innocency in

**Matthew 1:18–25**
Now the birth of Jesus Christ was as follows: After His mother Mary was betrothed to Joseph, before they came together, she was found with child of the Holy Spirit. Then Joseph her husband, being a just *man*, and not wanting to make her a public example, was minded to put her away secretly. But while he thought about these things, behold, an angel of the Lord appeared to him in a dream, saying, "Joseph, son of David, do not be afraid to take to you Mary your wife, for that which is conceived in her is of the Holy Spirit. And she will bring forth a Son, and you shall call His name JESUS, for He will save His people from their sins." Now all this was done that it might be fulfilled which was spoken by the Lord through the prophet, saying: "*Behold, the virgin shall be with child, and bear a Son, and they shall call His name Immanuel,*" which is translated, "God with us." Then Joseph, being aroused from sleep, did as the angel of the Lord commanded him and took to him his wife, and did not know her till she had brought forth her firstborn Son. And he called His name JESUS.

the matter and naturally assumes that Mary has been sexually unfaithful; thus, he plans to divorce her.

- An angel (messenger) from the Lord (1:20) explains to Joseph what has really occurred—what is conceived in her is from the Holy Spirit.
- Probably it is the angel (1:22–23) who explains to him that the birth of Jesus is the fulfilment of the prophecy in Isaiah 7:14: "the virgin shall conceive and bear a Son." The Hebrew word for "virgin" in this verse—'almâh—clearly indicates a young woman who had never experienced sexual relations with a man.
- Joseph (1:24) believes the angel's explanation, obeys his instructions and takes the pregnant, virgin Mary home to be his wife.
- Mary's virginity continues until after she gives birth to a son (1:25).

In Luke's account, we also learn the following facts:

- God sends the angel Gabriel (1:26–27) to a virgin who is pledged to be married to a man named Joseph. The virgin's name is Mary. Twice it is mentioned that she is "a virgin," which in the context indicates that she is unmarried and chaste.
- Mary is told (1:31) that she will be with child (pregnant) and give birth to a son. She protests (1:34) that this is impossible since she has not known a man—she has not had sexual intercourse. Mary claims to

be a virgin.

- The angel explains (1:35) that the conception of this child will take place by the Holy Spirit and the power of the Most High God. The birth of this child will be supernatural.

### Why the virgin birth?

One traditional explanation for this method of the entry of Jesus into the world was that it preserved Jesus from original sin, the result of Adam's fall. This explanation is unsatisfactory. Although it rules out the male donor from the equation, it leaves in female participation in the birth of Jesus. Jesus could have acquired original sin from Mary just as well as from Joseph.

It might be argued that Mary was chosen because of an inherent moral or spiritual superiority that made her stand out among her contemporaries. But Mary, like the rest of mankind, was a sinner in need of redemption.

The virgin birth must be seen as nothing less than a miracle in which the Holy Spirit prevented the passage of sin to the Lord Jesus from his fallen mother. Also, the virgin birth is God's fulfillment of what is known as the Davidic Covenant, which God brought about in the fullness of time.

### The Davidic Covenant

The Apostle Paul writes that the time of Jesus Christ's birth occurred in the fullness of time (Galatians 4:4). In other words, in God's sovereign economy, the march of history

**Galatians 4:4**
But when the fullness of the time had come, God sent forth his Son, born of a woman, born under the law.

had been orchestrated for this specific moment and for this specific event. All the human elements necessary for the unfolding plan of redemption were perfectly collected. The long anticipation of a promised Messiah would finally come to an end.

That anticipation is well described in 2 Samuel 7:12. This is the passage that is commonly referred to as the Davidic Covenant. David had taken upon himself the goal of building God a permanent place of worship, the Temple, in Jerusalem. But then Nathan the prophet had a dream in which God rebuked David for his plans to build a house for God. The earthly king is reminded of God's faithfulness to Israel during Israel's forty-year sojourn in the wilderness. Yet God goes on to declare that a future descendant of David will be involved in building a house for God.

As it turns out, David's son, Solomon, will erect the first Temple in Jerusalem. However, there is an added prophetic element within God's decree that foresees a double fulfillment. The Messiah would be a direct descendant from David and he will build the ultimate and final Temple. His will be an everlasting kingdom.

**2 Samuel 7:12–13**
"When your days are fulfilled and you rest with your fathers, I will set up your seed after you, who will come from your body, and I will establish his kingdom. He shall build a house for My name, and I will establish the throne of his kingdom forever."

### David's house childless?

**Jeremiah 22:30**
"Thus says the LORD: 'Write this man down as childless, A man *who* shall not prosper in his days; For none of his descendants shall prosper, Sitting on the throne of David, And ruling anymore in Judah.'"

But in Jeremiah 22:30 we read that none of David's descendants shall prosper, or sit on the throne of David or rule in Judah. When the prophet Jeremiah uttered these words from God more than four centuries had passed since the time of David. They are in reference to King Jehoiachin and his descendants.

Jehoiachin was considered evil in the sight of God. He was one of the ruling monarchs of the Southern Kingdom during the days of the prophet Jeremiah. It was during this period that Babylon destroyed the nation and took many captives into exile, including the prophet Daniel. The final curse upon the Davidic monarchy was that no blood descendant of Jehoiachin would receive God's blessing. This poses a severe problem in light of the prophecy given in 2 Samuel 7 since Jehoiachin was a blood descendant of David (see the genealogies of Jesus in Matthew 1:1–16; Luke 3:23–31).

### The genealogies of Jesus

In the two genealogies of Jesus, Matthew and Luke give a detailed lineage of the ancestors of Jesus. What is extraordinary is that the two genealogies have clear differences and yet both have an important similarity. The genealogy in Matthew's account traces the bloodline of Joseph back to King David through David's son Solomon. This is also the line in which Jehoiachin appears. Now, Jeremiah recorded that no one from the line of Jehoiachin would sit on the throne of David. Is this a contradiction of the prophecy given to the prophet Nathan during the reign of David?

In the second genealogy, the one recorded in Luke, Luke also notes that Jesus traces his descent back to King David. However, unlike the Matthean passage, Luke mentions that his descent comes through David's other son

Nathan. In this line, God does not curse any of Nathan's descendants. Most commentators believe that this genealogy is a record of Mary's ancestors. Both Mary and Joseph have royal blood coursing through their veins. The difference is that no one from Joseph's family tree is an eligible candidate to reign as Messiah. God had so decreed in the time of Jeremiah.

## Implications of the virgin birth

The virgin birth is a declaration of God's sovereignty. God had to orchestrate the seemingly infinite details to preserve both bloodlines. Mary and Joseph were not haphazard choices; nor were they chosen because of some intrinsic merit on their part.

The virgin birth is also a declaration of God's faithfulness to his Covenant. God had decreed that the Messiah would be identified with a certain race (Israel); with a certain bloodline (David); through a specific method (virgin, see Isaiah 7:14). At the same time God did not violate his own decree when he eliminated the descendants of Jehoiachin as possible candidates.

Finally, the virgin birth is a unique and miraculous event in the unfolding history of redemption. It is a miraculous work of the Holy Spirit. It legitimizes the rightful place of Jesus as the King of the Jews through bloodline. It also enables Jesus to be our Saviour, for he shared in all of our humanity, though without sin.

**Isaiah 7:14**
"Therefore the Lord Himself will give you a sign: Behold, the virgin shall conceive and bear a Son, and shall call His name Immanuel."

[Jesus] touched the leper, and he touched the [funeral] bier, and yet he was undefiled. He had God's relationship to sin. He knew good and evil, but was in divine supremacy over it; knowing such things as God knows them. Had he been other than he was, these touches of the bier and of the leper would have defiled him. He must have been put outside the camp, and gone through the cleansing which the law prescribed. But nothing of this kind do we see in him. He...was not merely undefiled, he was undefilable; and yet, such was the mystery of his person, such the perfection of the manhood in company with the Godhead in him, that the temptation was as real in him as was the undefilableness.

*John Gifford Bellett (1795–1864)*

# 4 The sinless life of Christ
Heinz G. Dschankilic

The truth of the incarnation of Jesus Christ has two sides to it: Jesus Christ is fully God and Jesus Christ is fully man. The evidence for the first assertion can be seen throughout the New Testament.[1] The New Testament also bears witness to another side of Christ, though—his humanity. As Paul puts it in 1 Timothy 2:5, he is "the *man* Christ Jesus" (italics added), and throughout the gospel records his humanity is evident:

- He experienced the pangs of hunger (Matthew 4:2).
- He knew weariness and thirst (John 4:6–7; 19:28).
- He wept genuine tears of sorrow (John 11:35).
- He went through human weakness and agony (Luke 22:43–44).
- He bled and died (John 19:34–37).

**Matthew 4:2**
And when He had fasted forty days and forty nights, afterward He was hungry.

**John 11:35**
Jesus wept.

**Luke 22:43–44**
Then an angel appeared to Him from heaven, strengthening Him. And being in agony, He prayed more earnestly. And His sweat became like great drops of blood falling down to the ground.

Yet, while his humanness is so like ours in all of these aspects, there is one way in which it is totally unlike that of any other man or woman: it is sinless.

## Christ never committed a sin
This affirmation first of all means that Christ

[1] See Chapter 1.

never *actually* committed a sin

In the words of 1 Peter 2:22, Christ "committed no sin." As we look at his life as it is recorded in the four Gospels, there is not one incident to which we can point and say, "Look, a sin." We never hear him asking for forgiveness, from God or from man.

In fact, he can pointedly state in John 8:46a: "Which of you convicts Me of sin?" This question speaks of a conscience that is clear of sin and in unbroken fellowship with God the Father.

During the moments leading up to his passion, Christ makes a similar declaration when he states that "the ruler of this world is coming, and he has nothing in Me" (John 14:30b). The devil has no claim upon Christ, for Christ has never sinned.

**2 Corinthians 5:21**
For He made Him who knew no sin *to be* sin for us, that we might become the righteousness of God in Him.

In 2 Corinthians 5:21, the Apostle Paul bears his own witness to this fact of Christ's never having sinned when he states that Christ "knew no sin." Here, Paul is affirming that Christ did not gain or acquire a knowledge of human sinfulness by acts of sin.

### Christ did not have sinful nature

But we must go further and affirm that the sinlessness of Jesus also means that Christ did not possess a nature bent and warped by the presence of sin. In Christ there was no *inherent* sin:

- 1 Peter 1:19 affirms that he was "without blemish and without spot," that is, blameless and free from vice.

- 1 John 3:5 asserts that "in Him there is no sin."
- Hebrews 7:26 describes him as one *"who is holy, harmless, undefiled, separate from sinners."*

In other words, Christ had no inner compulsion or desire to engage in sin. He always delighted in the will of God and in holiness. As he said in John 4:34: "My food is to do the will of Him who sent Me, and to finish His work."

In the Sermon on the Mount Jesus tells us that "the pure in heart...shall see God" (Matthew 5:8). But he is the one who has an unclouded vision of God. Read John 1:18. The Son is able to speak fully and clearly about the Father because he has an unswerving sight of the Father. As one reads the New Testament it is unthinkable to suppose that Jesus' vision of God was ever dim or cloudy. Otherwise how could he have ever responded to Philip's desire for the vision of God with this remarkable statement: "He who has seen Me has seen the Father" (John 14:9b). Jesus can give the vision of God to sinners because he alone has a completely unobstructed sight of God and his glory.

**John 1:18**
No one has seen God at any time. The only begotten Son, who is in the bosom of the Father, He has declared Him.

The Scriptures, therefore, deny not only the presence of sinful thinking and acts in the incarnate Christ, but also any ultimate roots of sin, as well as any inclinations, however latent and rudimentary, toward sin. The words of James 1:14–15, which indicate that every man and woman is tempted to sin by

**James 1:14–15**
But each one is tempted when he is drawn away by his own desires and enticed. Then, when desire has conceived, it gives birth to sin; and sin, when it is full-grown, brings forth death.

an inner inclination toward sin, do not apply to Christ. It is our lusts that suggest, motivate and propel us into sin. But Christ knows nothing of this. To say that Christ had sinful inclinations is to assert nothing less than that Christ himself was in need of a Saviour! In other words, Christ *could* not sin.

## The temptations of Jesus—were they real?

Hebrews 4:15
For we do not have a High Priest who cannot sympathize with our weaknesses, but was in all *points* tempted as *we are, yet* without sin.

What then of the temptations that came Jesus' way: were they real? We read of them, of course, in the Gospel accounts and in a passage like Hebrews 4:15. Christ knows our frame intimately, for he has stood where we stand, yet "without sin." As a current writer has noted, just as an Olympic weightlifter who successfully lifts and holds over head the heaviest weight in the games feels the force of it more fully than one who attempts to lift it and drops it, so it was with Christ's experience of temptation.[2] He faced every temptation to the very end and triumphed over them all. He felt the force and fury of them in a way that the rest of humanity, who regularly fall in the face of temptation, have not.

## Christ's humanity and his sinlessness

The importance of Christ's sinlessness is seen in the book of Hebrews. The theme of this book is the superiority of Christ. The writer of this magnificent epistle goes to great lengths to show that the New Covenant, established by Jesus Christ, is far and away superior to the Old Covenant that has now been fulfilled.

2 Wayne Grudem, *Systematic Theology. An Introduction to Biblical Doctrine* (Leicester: Inter-Varsity Press/Grand Rapids: Zondervan Publishing House, 1994), 539.

The most significant holy day in the calendar of the Old Covenant was the Day of Atonement. It was a day in which the nation as a whole sought to propitiate the wrath and anger of Yahweh against whom they had sinned.

Two things about the sacrifices on this day are noteworthy. First, the priests responsible for carrying out the sacrifices were themselves not exempt from appeasing God's wrath for their own sin. For example, before Aaron was allowed to perform the sacrifice necessary to atone for the nation's sin, he first had to kill a bull in order to atone for his personal sin and the sin of his household. Once this requirement was fulfilled, a second sacrifice could then be offered on behalf of the nation (Leviticus 16:6–10).

Second, the quality of the sacrifice that was being offered needs to be noted. Although not explicitly mentioned in Leviticus 16, there are hosts of examples within the Old Testament that describe the characteristics of a sacrifice. The key component was that the victim could not have any physical defects (Leviticus 3:1; 14:10).

### Christ: the spotless Priest

In Hebrews it is clearly stated that Christ is both the utterly spotless Priest *and* the completely innocent victim.

Christ's priesthood, based partly on his full identification with the human condition, enables Christ to act as a sympathetic and merciful High Priest who can make propitiation

**Leviticus 16:6–10**
"Aaron shall offer the bull as a sin offering, which *is* for himself, and make atonement for himself and for his house. He shall take the two goats and present them before the LORD *at* the door of the tabernacle of meeting. Then Aaron shall cast lots for the two goats: one lot for the LORD and the other lot for the scapegoat. And Aaron shall bring the goat on which the LORD's lot fell, and offer it *as* a sin offering. But the goat on which the lot fell to be the scapegoat shall be presented alive before the LORD, to make atonement upon it, and to let it go as the scapegoat into the wilderness."

**Leviticus 3:1**
'When his offering is a sacrifice of a peace offering, if he offers *it* of the herd, whether male or female, he shall offer it without blemish before the LORD.'

**Leviticus 14:10**
"And on the eighth day he shall take two male lambs without blemish, one ewe lamb of the first year without blemish, three-tenths *of an ephah* of fine flour mixed with oil as a grain offering, and one log of oil."

**Hebrews 2:17**
Therefore, in all things He had to be made like *His* brethren, that He might be a merciful and faithful High Priest in things *pertaining* to God, to make propitiation for the sins of the people.

**Hebrews 4:15**
For we do not have a High Priest who cannot sympathize with our weaknesses, but was in all *points* tempted as *we are, yet* without sin.

**Hebrews 7:26–27**
For such a High Priest was fitting for us, *who is* holy, harmless, undefiled, separate from sinners, and has become higher than the heavens; who does not need daily, as those high priests, to offer up sacrifices, first for His own sins and then for the people's, for this He did once for all when He offered up Himself.

for the sins of his people (Hebrews 2:17). But unlike the Aaronic priests, Christ needed no atonement for his own sin for, as we have seen, Christ was totally without sin.

Although Christ identifies with human temptation, having suffered and died on our behalf (Hebrews 2:18), the writer is quick to point out Christ's utter sinlessness (Hebrews 4:15). In the Old Covenant, for an animal sacrifice to be deemed acceptable it would need to be free from any physical defect. It needed to be perfect. Christ's utter sinlessness transcends mere physical purity. His purity is a complete and total spiritual purity; therefore, by virtue of his sinless condition, he can take upon himself the punishment reserved for the wicked (Hebrews 2:9).

Christ's sinless Priesthood and utter purity as a sacrifice means that he can be the mediator of a better covenant, in which there no longer needs to be continual sacrifice for sin (Hebrews 7:26–27).

Consequently, atonement for the child of God is final, ultimate and complete (Hebrews 10:10).

I do believe that we slander Christ when we think we are to draw the people by something else other than the preaching of Christ crucified.

*Charles Haddon Spurgeon (1834–1892)*


[The crucifixion of Christ is] the most solemn spectacle in all history, a spectacle unparalleled, unique, unrepeated, and unrepeatable. ...Here we are the spectators of a wonder the praise and glory of which eternity will not exhaust. It is the Lord of glory, the Son of God incarnate, the God-man, drinking the cup given him by the eternal Father, the cup of woe and of indescribable agony....It is God in our nature forsaken of God. The cry from the accursed tree evinces nothing less than the abandonment that is the wages of sin. And it was abandonment endured vicariously because he bore our sins in his own body on the tree.

*John Murray (1898–1975)*

# 5   The crucified Christ
Don Theobald

The theme of the Bible and the heart of the gospel is the death of our Lord Jesus Christ on the cross for sinners. A proper understanding of this great doctrine will produce increased faith, love, worship, godliness and obedience in the life of the believer. Christ crucified must be the focal point of our preaching and witnessing. It is the work of Christ on the cross that saves sinners. It is also the cross that is a stumbling block and foolishness for sinners (1 Corinthians 1:23–25). The truth of the crucified Christ is the target of attack by the enemies of the gospel and by Satan himself.

**1 Corinthians 1:23-25**
...but we preach Christ crucified, to the Jews a stumbling block and to the Greeks foolishness, but to those who are called, both Jews and Greeks, Christ the power of God and the wisdom of God. Because the foolishness of God is wiser than men, and the weakness of God is stronger than men.

## The necessity of the cross

The nature and character of God makes Christ's dying on the cross a necessity. God is holy (Isaiah 6:3; Revelation 4:8) and he is too pure to look on evil (Habakkuk 1:13). His wrath is being revealed from heaven against all the godlessness and wickedness of men (Romans 1:18). God also is a righteous judge, a God who expresses his wrath every day (Psalm 7:11).

The cross is also necessary because of the nature and condition of people (Psalm 51:5; Isaiah 53:6; Romans 3:23). We are, because of our sin, separated from the life of God

**Psalm 51:5**
Behold, I was brought forth in iniquity, And in sin my mother conceived me.

**Isaiah 53:6**
All we like sheep have gone astray; We have turned, every one, to his own way; And the LORD has laid on Him the iniquity of us all.

**Romans 3:23**
...for all have sinned and fall short of the glory of God.

(Ephesians 4:18), alienated from God and enemies in our minds (Colossians 1:21), under
condemnation (Romans 5:18) and destined
for hell (Matthew 23:33). Because of who God
is and because of who people are, it is absolutely necessary that the sinless Son of God had to
die on the cross as a sacrifice for sinners.

### The Old Testament background

The death of Jesus on the cross recorded in
the Gospels was prepared for, prefigured by
and predicted in the Old Testament. An altar
as a place of sacrifice and worship was essential to the patriarchs in Genesis (12:8;
22:1–14; 26:25; 46:1). Under the Mosaic
Covenant, a variety of sacrifices and offerings
constituted Israel's worship, culminating in
the Day of Atonement (Leviticus 16:1–24;
23:26–32). Numerous Old Testament prophe-
cies and predictions pointed ahead to that
time when the Christ would lay down his life
for his people (Isaiah 53:1–12).

### The nature of the cross

The cross is based on the person (who he is)
and work (what he came to do) of our Lord
Jesus Christ. Jesus' life, perfectly lived under
the Law (Hebrews 5:7–10; Galatians 4:4–5;
1 Peter 2:22)—or his *active obedience*—
secured for his people a perfect righteousness
before a holy God. And his sacrificial
death—or his *passive obedience*—secured for
his people perfect pardon and forgiveness for
all their sins. Three aspects of the death of
Christ should be noted:

1) His death is voluntary.

The Son of Man came to serve and willingly give his life for others (Mark 10:45; John 10:17–18).

2) His death is vicarious.

Jesus died as the substitute in the place of sinners. He took their sins upon himself, and he died on their behalf (Isaiah 53:12; Romans 5:6–8; Galatians 1:4).

3) His death is penal.

In taking our place, Jesus endured the penalty for our sins. Though Jesus was personally and actually innocent, he was made officially guilty and was condemned and executed as a criminal. He incurred the punishment which his people legally deserved (Isaiah 53:1–12; Deuteronomy 21:22–23; Luke 23:38–41).

**The aspects of the cross**

The cross-work of Christ accomplished the following for believers:

- Propitiation—Jesus appeased, placated and satisfied the righteous wrath of God. God presented him as a propitiation through faith in his blood (Romans 3:25; Hebrews 5:9; 1 John 2:2; 4:10).
- Expiation—Jesus removed, took away our guilt by way of paying the penalty for our sin.
- Redemption—Jesus secured our release from the bondage of sin through the payment of a price (1 Timothy 2:6; 1 Peter 1:18–19).

**John 10:17–18**
"Therefore My Father loves Me, because I lay down My life that I may take it again. No one takes it from Me, but I lay it down of Myself. I have power to lay it down, and I have power to take it again. This command I have received from My Father."

**Isaiah 53:12**
Therefore I will divide Him a portion with the great, and He shall divide the spoil with the strong, because He poured out His soul unto death, and He was numbered with the transgressors, and He bore the sin of many, and made intercession for the transgressors.

**Romans 5:6–8**
For when we were still without strength, in due time Christ died for the ungodly. For scarcely for a righteous man will one die; yet perhaps for a good man someone would even dare to die. But God demonstrates His own love toward us, in that while we were still sinners, Christ died for us.

**Galatians 1:4**
[Christ] gave Himself for our sins, that He might deliver us from this present evil age, according to the will of our God and Father.

**1 Timothy 2:6**
...who gave Himself a ransom for all...

**1 Peter 1:18–19**
...knowing that you were not redeemed with...silver or gold... but with the precious blood of Christ, as of a lamb without blemish and without spot.

- Remission—Jesus, by his death, secured the removal or the sending away of all our sins (Hebrews 9:22).
- Reconciliation—the death of Jesus restored our relationship to God the Father (Romans 5:9–11).
- Justification—the death of Jesus changed our legal status before God, so that we are declared righteous in his sight (Romans 3:24; 11:33).

### The extent of the cross

The question now is for whom did Christ die? This is not a question of the sufficiency of Christ's death. Christ's death is of infinite value and is sufficient to save every person who ever lived or will live. The issue is what is the divine intention in terms of the purpose and design of the cross? There are two main answers within orthodox, evangelical Christianity:

1) Christ died for all the sins of everyone who has ever lived—he died to save the whole world.

2) Christ died for all the sins of all his people down through history—he died to save all the elect.

Although the Bible does use words like "all," "every," "the world" etc. in relation to the death of Christ, these words must be understood in their context. Because it is the cross and Christ crucified that secures the salvation of sinners, Christ must have died with a clear intention to save particular people, for not everyone is saved (Matthew 1:21; John 6:37–40; 10:15; Ephesians 5:25; Titus 2:14).

## The application of the cross

How does what Christ did at the cross two thousand years ago become personally applied to sinners? The answer is twofold. God must act upon sinners so that they will see their need of a Saviour and find that need met in Jesus Christ. God works through the Word of God and by the Holy Spirit (Romans 10:17; 2 Thessalonians 2:13; 1 Peter 1:23; James 1:18). But, individuals also must act and respond to the gospel. Sinners must exercise faith and repentance if they are to benefit from Christ crucified (Mark 1:14–15; John 3:16).

## The results of the cross

Some results of the cross are as follows:

- The triune God is glorified, worshipped and honoured (John 17:1–5; Revelation 5:9–14).
- Sinners are saved and restored to a right relationship to God (Romans 3:21–25; 5:1–5; 8:29).
- Satan, the number one enemy of God and people, is defeated, doomed and damned (John 12:31–33; Hebrews 2:14; 1 John 3:8; Revelation 20:7–10).
- There is renewal of the cosmic order. This world, which has been radically affected by Satan, and Adam's fall will be made new and whole again (Romans 8:19–21; 2 Peter 3:10–13; Revelation 21:1,22).

**Titus 2:14**
...who gave Himself for us, that He might redeem us from every lawless deed and purify for Himself *His* own special people, zealous for good works.

**Romans 10:17**
So then faith *comes* by hearing, and hearing by the word of God.

**2 Thessalonians 2:13**
But we are bound to give thanks to God always for you, brethren beloved by the Lord, because God from the beginning chose you for salvation through sanctification by the Spirit and belief in the truth.

**1 Peter 1:23**
...having been born again...through the word of God which lives and abides forever

**James 1:18**
Of His own will He brought us forth by the word of truth, that we might be a kind of first-fruits of His creatures.

**Mark 1:14–15**
Now after John was put in prison, Jesus came to Galilee, preaching the gospel of the kingdom of God, and saying, "The time is fulfilled, and the kingdom of God is at hand. Repent, and believe in the gospel."

**Hebrews 2:14b**
...that through death He might destroy him who had the power of death, that is, the devil.

**Revelation 21:22**
But I saw no temple in it, for the Lord God Almighty and the Lamb are its temple.

If Christ be risen from the dead, according to the Scriptures, then all that the Scripture declares of the necessity and design of his sufferings, of his present glory, and of his future advent, must be true likewise. What a train of weighty consequences depend upon his resurrection!

*John Newton (1725–1807)*

# 6   The risen Lord
Pierre Constant

The resurrection and ascension of Jesus constitute the cornerstone of the Christian faith. As the Apostle Paul notes, if Christ has not been raised from the dead, our preaching and our faith are useless, we are still in our sins, those who have fallen asleep in the Lord are lost, and we are to be pitied more than all men (1 Corinthians 15:14–19). But because Jesus was raised from the dead and is exalted to the right hand of God, our faith relies upon a foundation second to none!

## The reality of the death of Jesus

Read Matthew 28:5–6. Let us note that Jesus really died following his crucifixion: he was flogged, beaten, crowned with a crown of thorns and crucified. The reality of Jesus' death was evident in the following ways:

- A Roman soldier pierced his side with a spear to make sure he was dead (John 19:33–35).
- Pilate sent a Roman centurion to verify Jesus was dead before he gave the corpse away to Joseph of Arimathea (Mark 15:43–45).
- His body was wrapped in linen cloth in which were put a hundred pounds of perfume and then placed in a tomb where no one had yet been buried (Luke 23:53;

**Matthew 28:5–6**
But the angel answered and said to the women, "Do not be afraid, for I know that you seek Jesus who was crucified. He is not here; for He is risen, as He said. Come, see the place where the Lord lay."

**John 19:33–35**
But when they came to Jesus and saw that He was already dead, they did not break His legs. But one of the soldiers pierced His side with a spear, and immediately blood and water came out. And he who has seen has testified, and his testimony is true; and he knows that he is telling the truth, so that you may believe.

**Mark 15:43–45**
Joseph of Arimathea, a prominent council member, who was himself waiting for the kingdom of God, coming and taking courage, went in to Pilate and asked for the body of Jesus. Pilate marveled that He was already dead; and summoning the centurion, he asked him if He had been dead for some time. And when he found out from the centurion, he granted the body to Joseph.

**Luke 23:55**
And the women who had come with Him from Galilee followed after, and they observed the tomb and how His body was laid.

**Matthew 27:62-66**
On the next day, which followed the Day of Preparation, the chief priests and Pharisees gathered together to Pilate, saying, "Sir, we remember, while He was still alive, how that deceiver said, 'After three days I will rise.' Therefore command that the tomb be made secure until the third day, lest His disciples come by night and steal Him *away*, and say to the people, 'He has risen from the dead.' So the last deception will be worse than the first." Pilate said to them, "You have a guard; go your way, make *it* as secure as you know how." So they went and made the tomb secure, sealing the stone and setting the guard.

**Luke 24:12**
But Peter arose and ran to the tomb; and stooping down, he saw the linen cloths lying by themselves; and he departed, marveling to himself at what had happened.

**Matthew 28:9-10**
And as they went to tell His disciples, behold, Jesus met them, saying, "Rejoice!" And they came and held Him by the feet and worshiped Him. Then Jesus said to them, "Do not be afraid. Go *and* tell My brethren to go to Galilee, and there they will see Me."

John 19:39–40).

- Some of the female disciples of Jesus saw the precise location where the body was laid (Luke 23:55).
- The tomb was sealed with a stone and a Roman guard was posted to make sure the disciples would not come to steal the corpse and pretend later that Jesus was raised from the dead (Matthew 27:62–66).

The intensity of the sufferings of the crucifixion, the spear in Jesus' side, the way he was wrapped up in linen, the Roman guard outside the tomb and the stone which was sealed, all these attest to the certainty of the death of Jesus and to the impossibility that he had merely fainted, woke up later in the tomb, came out of the tomb after pushing aside the large stone and then escaped without being noticed by the soldiers.

### The resurrection of Jesus is attested

After three days in the tomb, Jesus rises from the dead (Matthew 28). This is confirmed by

- The empty tomb, as witnessed by Mary Magdalene (John 20:1) and the other Mary (Matthew 28:1), to whom angels announced Jesus was raised from the dead (Matthew 28:2–7; Mark 16:5–7; Luke 24:4–8), as well as by the Apostles Peter and John (Luke 24:12; John 20:3–10)
- The appearance of the risen Jesus to
  1) Mary Magdalene (John 20:11–18) and to the other Mary (Matthew 28:9–10)

2) the disciples on the way to Emmaus (Luke 24:13–31)
3) Simon Peter (Luke 24:34)
4) the eleven and those with them (Luke 24:36–43)
5) the Apostles while Thomas was absent (John 20:19–25) and to the Apostles eight days later (John 20:26–29)
6) seven disciples on the seashore in Galilee (John 21)
7) the eleven on a mountain in Galilee (Matthew 28:16–20)

Paul adds that Jesus appeared to Peter, to the twelve, to more than 500 brothers at the same time, to James and finally to himself (1 Corinthians 15:6–8). Luke notes that these manifestations took place during forty days (Acts 1:3). Finally, Jesus appeared to his disciples in Bethany, on the Mount of Olives, from where he was taken up into heaven (Luke 24:50–51; Acts 1:4–10). He was thus seen by witnesses whom God had already chosen and who knew him well (Acts 10:40–41). Those who did not believe Moses or the prophets were not given any special sign (Luke 16:27–31).

The religious authorities, though they pretended the disciples came and stole the body of Jesus during the night (Matthew 28:11–15), were never able to deny the facts, to stop the disciples (Acts 4:18–22), or to show Jesus' body, which would silence the claims of the disciples once and for all.

The transformed lives of the disciples also

John 20:19–25
Then, the same day at evening, being the first *day* of the week, when the doors were shut where the disciples were assembled, for fear of the Jews, Jesus came and stood in the midst, and said to them, "Peace be with you." When He had said this, He showed them *His* hands and His side. The disciples were glad when they saw the Lord. So Jesus said to them again, "Peace to you! As the Father has sent Me, I also send you." And when He had said this, He breathed on *them,* and said to them, "Receive the Holy Spirit. If you forgive the sins of any, they are forgiven them; if you retain the *sins* of any, they are retained." Now Thomas, called Didymus, one of the twelve, was not with them when Jesus came. The other disciples therefore said to him, "We have seen the Lord." But he said to them, "Unless I see in His hands the print of the nails, and put my finger into the print of the nails, and put my hand into His side, I will not believe."

bear witness to the resurrection of Jesus. These unschooled individuals (Acts 4:13), fearful and selfish, who abandoned Jesus the night just before his trial, became bold witnesses of the risen Jesus before the authorities and the people, even when facing persecution and death (Acts 4:18–31; 5:17–42; 12:1–2). Paul, who persecuted the followers of this new Way, was transformed and preached publicly Jesus' resurrection and faith in him (Acts 13:32–39; 22:1–16; 26:9–29). The resurrection of Jesus lies at the heart of the gospel message (Luke 24:45–48; Acts 2:22–32; 3:15; 4:10–12; 10:37–43; 13:32–39; 26:22–23; 1 Corinthians 15:1–11).

## Consequences of the resurrection of Jesus

The resurrection of Jesus is more than a historical fact and the object of our faith; it has resounding consequences in all domains of our lives (Colossians 1:18)!

The resurrection of Jesus supports his claims to be the only way to God. Indeed, if Jesus did not rise from the dead, he is then not different from the founders of other religious movements. But having been raised from the dead, he demonstrates that only in him can one find the way to God (Acts 4:10–12). Paul writes that Jesus was "delivered up because of our offenses, and was raised because of our justification" (Romans 4:25). Peter adds that God has given us new birth through the resurrection of Jesus Christ from the dead (1 Peter 1:3–4).

## The resurrection of Jesus testifies to his supreme authority

The resurrection of Jesus serves to testify to his supreme authority over

- all human religions (John 2:18–22)
- all his enemies (1 Corinthians 15:24–28)
- death itself (Acts 13:34; Romans 6:9 1 Corinthians 15:26).

He is the Lord of the living and the dead (Romans 14:9), the firstborn from the dead and the ruler of the kings of the earth (Revelation 1:5,18).

An essential element of the gospel message (1 Corinthians 15:1–11), the resurrection of Jesus is also the firstfruits and the guarantee of our own resurrection (Romans 8:11; 1 Corinthians 15:20–23; Philippians 3:20–21). Because Jesus came back to life, all those who believe in him and belong to him will rise from the dead into eternal life (1 Thessalonians 4:13–18).

## Impact of the resurrection on believers

For the Christian, the resurrection of Jesus

- drives us toward a holy life, freed from sin and its evil desires (1 Corinthians 6:14–17)
- drives us to forsake this world (2 Corinthians 5:15)
- sets our hearts on things above (Colossians 3:1)
- assures us that our labour is not in vain (1 Corinthians 15:58; Hebrews 13:20–21)

John 2:18–22
So the Jews answered and said to Him, "What sign do You show to us, since You do these things?" Jesus answered and said to them, "Destroy this temple, and in three days I will raise it up." Then the Jews said, "It has taken forty-six years to build this temple, and will You raise it up in three days?" But He was speaking of the temple of His body. Therefore, when He had risen from the dead, His disciples remembered that He had said this to them; and they believed the Scripture and the word which Jesus had said.

1 Corinthians 15:26
The last enemy *that* will be destroyed *is* death.

Romans 8:11
But if the Spirit of Him who raised Jesus from the dead dwells in you, He who raised Christ from the dead will also give life to your mortal bodies through His Spirit who dwells in you.

2 Corinthians 5:15
...and He died for all, that those who live should live no longer for themselves, but for Him who died for them and rose again.

**2 Timothy 2:8–10**
Remember that Jesus Christ, of the seed of David, was raised from the dead according to my gospel, for which I suffer trouble as an evil-doer, *even* to the point of chains; but the word of God is not chained. Therefore I endure all things for the sake of the elect, that they also may obtain the salvation which is in Christ Jesus with eternal glory.

**Romans 6:5–6,13,18**
For if we have been united together in the likeness of His death, certainly we also shall be *in the likeness* of *His* resurrection, knowing this, that our old man was crucified with *Him*, that the body of sin might be done away with, that we should no longer be slaves of sin. ...And do not present your members *as* instruments of unright-eousness to sin, but present yourselves to God as being alive from the dead, and your members as instruments of righteousness to God. ...And having been set free from sin, you became slaves of righteousness.

**1 Corinthians 15:20**
But now Christ is risen from the dead, *and* has become the firstfruits of those who have fallen asleep.

- equips us to endure suffering (2 Timothy 2:8–10)
- enables us to proclaim his Word without losing heart (2 Corinthians 4:13)

Because he lives forever, he saves completely those who come to God through him, and intercedes for us (Hebrews 7:25), a truth to which the exaltation of Jesus to the right hand of God is also related.

**Believing and proclaiming the resurrection**

To believe and proclaim the gospel of the risen Christ is to

- believe and proclaim a gospel that frees us from the power of sin (Romans 6:5–6,13,18)
- proclaim a new life where we can bear fruit thanks to the Spirit of the risen Christ who indwells us (Romans 8:11–16)
- be freed from all condemnation (Romans 8:34)
- know security and eternal consolation (1 Corinthians 15:20; 1 Thessalonians 4:13–18)

To know Jesus as Lord and to personally appropriate the benefits of his death and resurrection is to escape eternal condemnation and to have eternal life (Romans 10:9).

I like to remember that our Lord Jesus is gone [to heaven] in the entirety of his nature. His body is gone. He has not left his flesh in the grave. Jesus has carried with him his entire self, his whole humanity. Therein I do rejoice; for he has carried my nature to heaven with him: my heart is with him on his throne, and all my being longs to follow it. Jesus has taken our manhood into heaven. He is in heaven, our Adam, the representative of his people....We shall know him there if we have known him here.

*Charles Haddon Spurgeon (1834–1892)*

# 7 The ascended King

Pierre Constant

The Christian faith has often put the accent, and rightly so, on the death and resurrection of Jesus. It is through Jesus' death and resurrection that we receive forgiveness for our sins (Romans 4:24–25).

However, one cannot speak about the resurrection of Jesus without also mentioning his ascension to the right hand of God. If the death of Jesus is not significant apart from his resurrection, his resurrection would be incomplete apart from his exaltation to the right hand of the Father. Jesus has not only come back to life; he ascended to the Father's right hand in order to receive heavenly royalty and supreme authority. He was crowned King and Lord. He is now above all creatures, visible and invisible!

## The ascension of Jesus presupposed in the New Testament

Without always being mentioned explicitly, Jesus' ascension and heavenly status are often presupposed in the New Testament.

Some texts speak of Jesus being enthroned in heaven and having a priestly ministry on behalf of his own people. He prepares a place for them before coming back and taking them with him in glory (Matthew 16:27; 19:28;

**Matthew 16:27**
"For the Son of Man will come in the glory of His Father with His angels, and then He will reward each according to his works."

John 14:2–3
"In My Father's house are many mansions; if *it were* not *so*, I would have told you. I go to prepare a place for you. And if I go and prepare a place for you, I will come again and receive you to Myself; that where I am, *there* you may be also."

24:30–31; John 14:2–3). The risen and ascended Jesus appears to Saul of Tarsus (Acts 9:5). This same Jesus reassures Paul in Corinth and commands him to pursue his work (Acts 18:9), and later declares to Paul he will testify in Rome (Acts 23:11).

In the prologue of the fourth Gospel, John writes: "And the Word became flesh and dwelt among us, and we beheld His glory, the glory as of the only begotten of the Father, full of grace and truth" (John 1:14). Jesus asserts he comes from heaven (3:13; 6:38), he comes from the Father (8:42) to whom he also returns (7:33–34; 8:21–23,42; 16:5,28). He speaks of himself as the Son of man in glory who will send his angels to root out the weeds from the wheat (Matthew 13:40–41).

### The reality of the ascension of Jesus
The Scriptures clearly teach that Jesus ascended to heaven and sat at his Father's right hand.

Already during his earthly ministry, Jesus foretold both his resurrection and ascension.

Psalm 110:1
The LORD said to my Lord, "Sit at My right hand, Till I make Your enemies Your footstool."

Quoting from Psalm 110 where David's Lord is invited to sit at the right hand of God (Psalm 110:1; see Matthew 22:44–45; 26:64; Luke 20:41–44; 22:69) and from Psalm 118 where one reads that "the stone *which* the builders rejected" would become the corner-stone (Psalm 118:22–23; Mark 12:1–12; Luke 20:9–18), Jesus identifies this "Lord" and this "stone" with himself. These prophetic declarations were not fulfilled in the person of David, but rather in Jesus of

Nazareth (Acts 2:33–35). Moreover, these predictions concern not only Jesus' death and resurrection, but ultimately his ascension to the right hand of God (Acts 2:34–35; 4:10–11).

As he prays to his Father, Jesus refers to the glory which was previously his before coming to earth; the preexistence of the Son of man is thus joined to his return to a glory previously shared with his Father (John 17:5; see also 13:3). John goes so far as to write that the glory of God which Isaiah saw in the temple was in fact the one belonging to the preexistent Son (John 12:40–41)! The Gospels give a glimpse of this glory in the transfiguration of Jesus (Mark 9:2–3), an event which immediately follows the mention of the future glory of the Son of man in each of the Gospels (Matthew 16:27–17:2; Mark 8:38–9:3; Luke 9:27–29).

The risen Jesus did not remain on earth, but ascended into heaven. Among the Evangelists, Luke depicts most clearly the events surrounding the ascension of Jesus (Luke 24:50–51; Acts 1:3–11). Forty days after his resurrection, Jesus went up to heaven from the Mount of Olives (Acts 1:3,9–12) near Bethany (Luke 24:50). Jesus ascended while his disciples were with him and as he spoke about the coming of the Spirit upon them in order that they would be his witnesses unto the ends of the earth (Acts 1:8–9). One must take note that Matthew 28:18–20 does not refer to the ascension of Jesus, but rather to one of Jesus' previous appearances in Galilee.

**John 17:5**
"And now, O Father, glorify Me together with Yourself, with the glory which I had with You before the world was."

**Luke 24:50–51**
And He led them out as far as Bethany, and He lifted up His hands and blessed them. Now it came to pass, while He blessed them, that He was parted from them and carried up into heaven.

**Acts 1:8–9**
"But you shall receive power when the Holy Spirit has come upon you; and you shall be witnesses to Me in Jerusalem, and in all Judea and Samaria, and to the end of the earth." Now when He had spoken these things, while they watched, He was taken up, and a cloud received Him out of their sight.

**Acts 7:56**
..."Look! I see the heavens opened and the Son of Man standing at the right hand of God!"

It is Jesus in heaven, this time standing at the right hand of God, whom Stephen sees in a heavenly vision (Acts 7:56). The ascension of Jesus is an integral part of the mystery of godliness, that is, the gospel message, as Paul writes: "...[He] was manifested in the flesh...[and] received up in glory" (1 Timothy 3:16). It is Jesus previously dead but now alive and ascended into heaven who appears to John on the island of Patmos and who tells him that he holds "the keys of Hades and of Death" (Revelation 1:18).

## The consequences of the exaltation of Jesus

If the Gospels and Acts presuppose and describe the ascension of Jesus, the New Testament epistles provide us with its meaning and consequences. Just as the resurrection of Jesus has many implications for the entirety of our lives, the ascension of Jesus and his glorification likewise have profound consequences for the course of human history as well as for the eternal destiny of the whole universe.

**Ephesians 1:19–22**
...and what is the exceeding greatness of His power toward us who believe, according to the working of His mighty power which He worked in Christ when He raised Him from the dead and seated *Him* at His right hand in the heavenly *places*, far above all principality and power and might and dominion, and every name that is named, not only in this age but also in that which is to come. And He put all *things* under His feet, and gave Him *to be* head over all *things* to the church.

## The exaltation and authority of Jesus

Praise and power are given to Jesus in the following ways:

- Jesus is exalted to the right hand of God as supreme ruler of the universe, and especially of the chuch (Ephesians 1:19–22).
- Jesus received from the Father supreme authority in heaven and on earth (Matthew 28:18).
- Seated at the right hand of God, he is now

"above all principality and power and might and dominion, and every name that is named, not only in this age but also in that which is to come" (Ephesians 1:21; see also 1 Peter 3:22).

- It is Jesus exalted by God to the highest place in the universe who receives universal worship and who is confessed as "Lord" to the glory of God the Father (Philippians 2:9–11).
- As supreme head of the church, Jesus bestows upon it all the necessary gifts for its growth (Ephesians 4:10–16).

The writer of the Epistle to the Hebrews asserts this truth over and over:

- Jesus is seated "at the right hand of the Majesty on high" (Hebrews 1:3).
- Jesus is exalted high above the angels, having inherited a name superior to theirs, the name "Son" (Psalm 2:7; Hebrews 1:5), "God" (Psalm 45:7–8; Hebrews 1:8–9), "Lord" (Psalm 102:26; Hebrews 1:10), the "Lord" of Psalm 110:1 (Hebrews 1:13; 10:12–14).
- God has subjected to him the world to come (Psalm 8:6; Hebrews 2:5,8; 1 Corinthians 15:25–28), and crowned him with honour and glory (Hebrews 2:9).
- His presence before God makes him our merciful and faithful high priest "able to aid those who are tempted" (Hebrews 2:18).
- Having gone through the heavens, Jesus the Son of God enables us to approach the throne of grace (Hebrews 4:14–16; John 14:13).

**Hebrews 4:14–16**
Seeing then that we have a great High Priest who has passed through the heavens, Jesus the Son of God, let us hold fast *our* confession. For we do not have a High Priest who cannot sympathize with our weaknesses, but was in all *points* tempted as *we are, yet* without sin. Let us therefore come boldly to the throne of grace, that we may obtain mercy and find grace to help in time of need.

## The exaltation and salvation of Jesus

The ascension of Jesus to the right hand of his Father demonstrates that Jesus is the only way to God the Father. After he told his disciples he would depart and prepare a place for them, Jesus said to Thomas: "I am the way, the truth, and the life. No one comes to the Father except through Me" (John 14:6). Following a quotation from an Old Testament text referring to the resurrection and ascension of Jesus (Psalm 118:22), Peter declares: "Nor is there salvation in any other, for there is no other name under heaven given among men by which we must be saved" (Acts 4:12).

The ascension of Jesus is also linked to the forgiveness of sins (Acts 5:31). The Lord and Saviour whom the disciples preached is unlike any other: he died, rose from the dead and is exalted to the right hand of God!

## The assurance of salvation

The ascension of Jesus to the right hand of God also entails assurance of salvation for his chosen ones (Romans 8:34–35; Hebrews 7:25; 1 John 2:1–2). The assurance of our salvation is rooted in the resurrection and ascension of the Son of God. It is this Jesus who sat down at the right hand of God who is the author and perfecter of our faith (Hebrews 12:2)! No surprise, then, that we are called to hold firmly to the faith we profess because Jesus ascended into heaven (Hebrews 4:14).

## The coming of the Holy Spirit

The departure of Jesus means that he is no

**Psalm 118:22**
The stone *which* the builders rejected Has become the chief cornerstone.

**Acts 5:31**
"Him God has exalted to His right hand *to be* Prince and Savior, to give repentance to Israel and forgiveness of sins"

**Romans 8:34–35**
Who is he who condemns? *It is* Christ who died, and furthermore is also risen, who is even at the right hand of God, who also makes intercession for us. Who shall separate us from the love of Christ? *Shall* tribulation, or distress, or persecution, or famine, or nakedness, or peril, or sword?

longer physically present for his disciples, but it also means he is permanently and universally present by the Spirit he sent after he was taken up to heaven. After he sat at the right hand of God, he "received from the Father the promise of the Holy Spirit" and has poured him out upon his disciples (Acts 2:33). Indeed, according to the Gospel of John, the departure of Jesus is prerequisite to the coming of the Holy Spirit among the disciples of Jesus (John 7:39). See the testimony of Jesus himself about this in John 16:7.

John 16:7
"Nevertheless I tell you the truth. It is to your advantage that I go away; for if I do not go away, the Helper will not come to you; but if I depart, I will send Him to you."

### The exaltation of Jesus and eternal life

Dwelling in heaven, Jesus prepares a place for his own, he will come back and take them to be with him forever (John 14:2–3; 1 Thessalonians 4:17). Thus, our hope in Christ is not only to live eternally, but especially to live eternally in the presence of the Son and the Father. "Eternal life" does not consist in living forever, but to live *with* God forever. It does not so much refer to duration of life as to the spiritual nature of this life, to our everlasting presence with God.

1 Thessalonians 4:17
Then we who are alive *and* remain shall be caught up together with them in the clouds to meet the Lord in the air. And thus we shall always be with the Lord.

### Conclusion

Jesus has not forsaken his disciples. On the contrary, he is always present among them through the Holy Spirit whom he sent to them after he was taken up in glory. He is the Lord of the universe, the supreme ruler of the church, the high priest in the order of Melchizedek, the Son of God, God, Prince and Saviour. To him be all the glory!

The subject of the person and work of the Holy Spirit is always important for study, for he is the Third Person of the Holy Trinity. He indwells the Christian and guides and enables [him] every day. Whatever the Scriptures set forth [about him], and from whatever part, should be a primary concern for every Christian.

*Leon J. Wood (1918–1977)*

# 8 The person and work of the Holy Spirit

David Kay

## Who is the Holy Spirit?

He is the third person of the Godhead, the Holy Trinity, and has all the attributes of God. He is equal with the Father and the Son. His personhood is shown in such passages as Acts 5:3–4 and John 14:16.

The Scriptures make it plain that the three persons of the Trinity are to be differentiated. When the Lord Jesus Christ was baptized God the Father spoke from heaven, God the Son in his human-divine form was being baptized and God the Holy Spirit came down upon him in the form of a dove (Matthew 3:16; Mark 1:10; Luke 3:22). God the Holy Spirit has his own distinct identity within the Godhead.

**Acts 5:3–4**
But Peter said, "Ananias, why has Satan filled your heart to lie to the Holy Spirit and keep back *part* of the price of the land for yourself? While it remained, was it not your own? And after it was sold, was it not in your own control? Why have you conceived this thing in your heart? You have not lied to men but to God."

## The personality of the Holy Spirit

The personhood of the Holy Spirit is revealed in the following ways:

**Mark 1:10**
And immediately, coming up from the water, He saw the heavens parting and the Spirit descending upon Him like a dove.

- He has a will (1 Corinthians 12:11).
- He has knowledge (Romans 8:27).
- He has feeling (Ephesians 4:30).
- He proceeds as a person from the Father and the Son (John 15:26; Galatians 4:6).

**Romans 8:27**
Now He who searches the hearts knows what the mind of the Spirit *is*, because He makes intercession for the saints according to *the will of* God.

## The divinity of the Holy Spirit

The divinity of the Holy Spirit is revealed in

**Ephesians 4:30**
And do not grieve the Holy Spirit of God, by whom you were sealed for the day of redemption.

the following ways:

**Psalm 139:7**
Where can I go from
Your Spirit? Or where
can I flee from Your
presence?

**Hebrews 9:14**
...how much more shall
the blood of Christ,
who through the eternal
Spirit offered Himself
without spot to God,
cleanse your conscience
from dead works to
serve the living God?

- He is everywhere—he is omnipresent (Psalm 139:7).
- He is all-seeing—he is omniscient (John 16:13; 1 Corinthians 2:10–11).
- He is eternal (Hebrews 9:14).

## The work of the Holy Spirit

Generally speaking, the work of the Holy Spirit is to consummate or complete what has been brought into existence by the Son at the Father's command. His work can be observed in both of the Testaments of the Scriptures.

In the Old Testament, the Holy Spirit's work is revealed by the following:

**Genesis 1:1–2**
In the beginning God
created the heavens
and the earth. The
earth was without form,
and void; and darkness
*was* on the face of the
deep. And the Spirit of
God was hovering over
the face of the waters.

**Judges 3:10**
The Spirit of the LORD
came upon him, and he
judged Israel. He went
out to war, and the
LORD delivered Cushan-
Rishathaim king of
Mesopotamia into his
hand; and his hand
prevailed over Cushan-
Rishathaim.

- He was involved in the creation of the universe (Genesis 1:1–2; Psalm 104:30).
- He empowered men for specific tasks:
  1) craftsmanship (Exodus 31:2–3)
  2) judgment and leadership (Judges 3:10)
  3) kingship (in Old Testament times the Holy Spirit entered and left certain men—King Saul and King David are examples [1 Samuel 16:13–14])
  4) prophecy (2 Chronicles 15:1; Micah 3:8)
- He inspired men during the Old Testament and New Testament periods to write Scripture (2 Peter 1:21).

In the New Testament, the Holy Spirit's activity is evident in the following ways:

- The Lord Jesus Christ was conceived by his power (Luke 1:35).
- He raised the Lord Jesus Christ from the dead (Romans 8:11; 1 Peter 3:18).
- He regenerates and makes alive his elect (John 3:5–6; Titus 3:5–6).
- He convicts them of their sins (John 16:8).
- He assures believers of their salvation (Romans 8:15).
- He seals their salvation (2 Corinthians 1:21–22).
- He counsels and teaches believers (John 16:12–14).
- He helps believers to pray (Romans 8:26).
- He indwells believers (1 Corinthians 3:16–17).
- He calls believers to service (Acts 13:2–4).
- He works in the church (1 Corinthians 12:7–11).
- At conversion a believer is baptized in the Holy Spirit by Christ, uniting all believers into one body (Luke 3:16; 1 Corinthians 12:13).
- Believers are commanded to be "filled with the Spirit" (Ephesians 5:18–21).
- He sanctifies the believer, that is, he makes the believer to become more like the Lord Jesus Christ (Galatians 5:22–24).

**Titus 3:5–6**
...not by works of righteousness which we have done, but according to His mercy He saved us, through the washing of regeneration and renewing of the Holy Spirit, whom He poured out on us abundantly through Jesus Christ our Savior.

**2 Corinthians 1:21–22**
Now He who establishes us with you in Christ and has anointed us *is* God, who also has sealed us and given us the Spirit in our hearts as a guarantee.

**1 Corinthians 3:16–17**
Do you not know that you are the temple of God and *that* the Spirit of God dwells in you? If anyone defiles the temple of God, God will destroy him. For the temple of God is holy, which *temple* you are.

**Galatians 5:22–24**
But the fruit of the Spirit is love, joy, peace, longsuffering, kindness, goodness, faithfulness, gentleness, self-control. Against such there is no law. And those *who are* Christ's have crucified the flesh with its passions and desires.

The application of redemption begins with the sovereign efficacious summons on the part of God....In order that this call may be answered, and the blessings of the high calling of God enjoyed, the inward supernatural regeneration and renewal of the Spirit is necessary...This change of heart manifests itself in faith and repentance, which are the responses of our whole inner man to the revelation of the Gospel, away from sin and towards God....Justification is that aspect of the application of redemption whereby God delivers us from condemnation, and accepting us as righteous in his sight receives us into his favour and fellowship.

*John Murray (1898–1975)*

# 9 The new birth and justification by faith

Jerry Marcellino

When our Lord Jesus Christ was secretly approached by Nicodemus, the teacher of Israel, he made it abundantly clear to him that all who will have eternal life must first experience the new birth. He taught him that all who will be called God's true people must experience a spiritual re-birth. Put simply, our Lord stated, they must be "born again" (John 3:1–8). Our Lord's reason for pressing this non-negotiable mandate was, and still is, because all men and women are physically born into this fallen world spiritually dead in their trespasses and sins (Ephesians 2:1). They are, "by nature children of wrath, just as the others" (Ephesians 2:3). This sad spiritual condition renders men and women totally unable to appraise or accept the spiritual things of the living God (1 Corinthians 2:14).

> **1 Corinthians 2:14**
> But the natural man does not receive the things of the Spirit of God, for they are foolishness to him; nor can he know *them*, because they are spiritually discerned.

Therefore, the non-Christian cannot and will not seek Christ for salvation apart from the initiating work of God the Holy Spirit (Romans 3:11; Philippians 1:6). He has no desire or ability to make the first move toward his salvation! We learn, then, that the greatest spiritual obstacle the unbeliever must face, in regard to his eternal welfare, is himself (Jeremiah 17:9). His human nature has produced a heart of stone (Ezekiel 36:26–27)

> **Jeremiah 17:9**
> "The heart is deceitful above all *things*, And desperately wicked; Who can know it?"

John 3:19–20
"And this is the condemnation, that the light has come into the world, and men loved darkness rather than light, because their deeds were evil. For everyone practicing evil hates the light and does not come to the light, lest his deeds should be exposed."

through his sinful inheritance at conception (Psalm 51:5) and at birth (Psalm 58:3). This explains why we should not be surprised that every son of Satan (John 8:44) is naturally in love with his sin and hates the light of God's special revelation (John 3:19–20).

We see, then, the scriptural and spiritual necessity for this doctrine of the new birth. We now understand why all men and women must experience a supernatural, God-authored, regenerative work in their life, or else, eternally perish in their sins (Hebrews 12:1–2; John 3:16).

### The doctrine of the new birth

Some important truths about the new birth:

John 3:1–2
There was a man of the Pharisees named Nicodemus, a ruler of the Jews. This man came to Jesus by night and said to Him, "Rabbi, we know that You are a teacher come from God; for no one can do these signs that You do unless God is with him."

- The new birth is a necessity (John 3:1–8) because men and women are
  1) utterly insensitive to spiritual matters (John 3:1–2; Ecclesiastes 3:11; Romans 1:18–20; 2:14–16)
  2) totally unable to respond to God in their own strength (John 3:5; Psalm 110:3; John 6:29,44,65; Romans 9:16; 10:13,17)
  3) born with a nature that is bent away from God, averse to holiness and inclined to sin (John 3:7; Romans 3:11,23; 5:12)
- The new birth is mysterious (John 3:4,8) because
  1) it is accomplished by the Holy Spirit, who acts when and upon whom he desires
  2) the Holy Spirit cannot be fully predicted
  3) the Holy Spirit is an utterly free agent who cannot be controlled

- The new birth is produced and brought into being by the Holy Spirit (John 3:6).

## Justification by faith alone

We now can grasp why every unbeliever must be raised from the spiritual graveyard or else perish in eternal hellfire (Luke 16:19–31). The Apostle Paul affirms this truth in Colossians 2:13.

This spiritual resurrection ensures that God's people will be justified by faith (Romans 3:24), and thus, declared not guilty in the high court of heaven. Thus, the doctrine of justification guarantees that every believer becomes the recipient of Christ's very own righteousness (2 Corinthians 5:21; Romans 1:17) at the moment of his or her salvation. We are saved by God's righteousness! In summary:

- God's righteousness is unobtainable through the work of man (Romans 3:21; Genesis 15:6; Habakkuk 2:4).
- God's righteousness is available to everyone who believes (Romans 3:22–23; John 3:16; Romans 10:12).
- God's righteousness is made possible only through the cross (Romans 3:24–26; 6:23; 8:33–34; 1 Corinthians 6:20; 2 Corinthians 5:21; Galatians 4:4; Ephesians 2:8–9; 2 Peter 3:9; 1 John 2:2).

This amazing truth is good news for sinful man—the sinner is justified freely by the gift of faith and, then, is treated by God as if he had never sinned! He is treated as one who is

**Colossians 2:13**
And you, being dead in your trespasses and the uncircumcision of your flesh, He has made alive together with Him, having forgiven you all trespasses...

**Romans 3:21–26**
But now the righteousness of God apart from the law is revealed, being witnessed by the Law and the Prophets, even the righteousness of God through faith in Jesus Christ, to all and on all who believe. For there is no difference; for all have sinned and fall short of the glory of God, being justified freely by His grace through the redemption that is in Christ Jesus, whom God set forth *as* a propitiation by His blood, through faith, to demonstrate His righteousness, because in His forbearance God had passed over the sins that were previously committed, to demonstrate at the present time His righteousness, that He might be just and the justifier of the one who has faith in Jesus.

legally innocent before God, no longer under the condemnation of God (Romans 8:1) and at peace with God (Romans 5:1). Justification is the free gift of God's abounding grace (Ephesians 2:8–9).

**Romans 5:1**
Therefore, having been justified by faith, we have peace with God through our Lord Jesus Christ.

## Conclusion

If you are a true believer, then you have received a new heart and have been raised from the dead. Go live as one who has been given new life (Ezekiel 36:26–27; Colossians 3:1–3).

If you have received the very righteousness of Jesus Christ through faith, go live a righteous life of faith (Matthew 5:6; Romans 1:16–17; Hebrews 11:6).

If your salvation is totally a work of God, then go work out your salvation to the glory of God (Isaiah 26:12; Ephesians 2:10; Philippians 2:12–13; 3:8–9).

The serene, silent beauty of a holy life is the most powerful influence in the world, next to the might of the Spirit of God.

*Charles Haddon Spurgeon (1834–1892)*

The greatest saints of God...have been intensely human and lovable people with a twinkle in their eyes.

*James Philip (1922– )*

# 10 Sanctification
Stephen Kring

We begin life as sinners, far from God, having lost our likeness to him given at creation, and completely unfit for his holy presence. It is against this dark background of such deficiencies that the saving truth of sanctification shines so brightly.

## Definition
The root meaning behind the words "sanctification," "sanctify," "saint," "holiness" and "holy" is "set apart." Therefore, sanctification takes place when our holy God sets apart unworthy sinners to be his own possession, by washing, purifying and cleansing them from sin through the atoning work of the Lord Jesus Christ on the cross, so that they will draw near to him, and by drawing near will come to know him and become like him.

## The biblical foundation of this doctrine
God, in himself, is absolutely holy. He is the altogether separate One. This is seen in his transcendence over all creation. It is also evident in his uniqueness. There is no other being, real or imagined, that equals him. God is also beyond comparison in his purity. He is the thrice-holy God (Exodus 15:11; 1 Samuel 2:2; Isaiah 6:3; 40:25; 45:5,6,21–22;

**Exodus 15:11**
"Who *is* like You, O LORD, among the gods? Who *is* like You, glorious in holiness, Fearful in praises, doing wonders?"

**Isaiah 6:3**
And one cried to another and said: "Holy, holy, holy *is* the LORD of hosts; The whole earth *is* full of His glory!"

Habakkuk 1:13; 1 John 1:5).

God's desire for a holy people was not satisfied by Adam and the old creation. For his own glory and his people's enjoyment, God wanted a people who would draw near to him, be with him, behold his glory and reflect his likeness. However, because of the fall of Adam into sin, he could not continue in God's presence. Likewise, Adam's unholy offspring proved to be unfit for this privileged position (Genesis 3:8,23–24; 6:5–6).

God's desire for a holy people was not satisfied by Israel under the Old Covenant. God chose and called Israel from among all the nations of the earth to become his holy people. Within Israel God set apart the tribe of Levi to act as priests and within the tribe of Levi, the family of Aaron to provide the High Priest. This priesthood then had the task of continually sanctifying the people, through various blood sacrifices as well as washings and sprinklings with water and oil. But all of these purifying processes could not touch the sinful hearts and consciences of the Old Covenant nation. In heart they remained unholy (Exodus 19:5–6,10,14; 30:25–33; Leviticus 8:12; 16:15–16; 19:2; Psalm 148:13–14; Ezra 10:8,13,18–19; Hebrews 9:9,13; 10:11).

**Hebrews 10:11**
And every priest stands ministering daily and offering repeatedly the same sacrifices, which can never take away sins.

So God chose, called and set apart his own beloved Son, Jesus. He was the tribe of Levi, the house of Aaron, the tabernacle, the temple, the altar, all of the sacrifices, the blood, the oil and the water all rolled up into one! He accomplished, by his atoning death on the cross, the cleansing, washing and purifying of his people that would effectually set them apart from their sins unto God once and forever. Through union with Christ by faith, God's New Covenant people, his new creation, his church is immediately regarded as holy. This holiness, through the cleansing work of Christ, results in a drawing near to God, a delight in his presence and glory and a desire to become like him. Thus a practical separation from sin and following after godliness ensues. This is ultimately consummated at the second coming of our Lord Jesus Christ when God's people will be perfectly conformed to the likeness of their Saviour. Then for all eternity God will have and be with his own special, holy people (Isaiah 49:5–6; John 10:36; 17:19; 1 Peter 2:9–10; Hebrews 9:12–14; Revelation 21:3)

**Revelation 21:3**
And I heard a loud voice from heaven saying, "Behold, the tabernacle of God *is* with men, and He will dwell with them, and they shall be His people and God Himself will be with them *and be* their God."

### Sanctification—a past event

There is a sense in which our sanctification is a past event:

- We are sanctified by the atoning death of Jesus Christ on the cross that cleanses us from all sin. He consecrates us to God thoroughly, inwardly, permanently, once for all time (Colossians 1:21–22; Hebrews 10:10,14; 13:12).
- We are therefore sanctified by faith. That is, the sanctifying effects of Christ's sacrifice are received when a sinner first trusts in him as Saviour (Acts 26:18).
- It is by believing the truth of the word of

the gospel through the working of the Holy Spirit that we are sanctified. Hence, sanctification is by the truth, through the Word, and of the Spirit (John 17:17,19; Ephesians 5:26; 2 Thessalonians 2:13; 1 Peter 1:2).

- Every sinner who is savingly joined to Christ by faith is immediately set apart by God for himself. He is sanctified. He takes his place among the saints (1 Corinthians 1:2,30; 6:11).

### Sanctification—a present process

Along with the inestimable blessing of being cleansed and consecrated to God as his own people comes the privilege and responsibility of becoming more and more a reflection of God himself. We are called to separate from sin and become like God in every area of our lives. Our attitudes will change. Our speech will be affected. Our conduct will be altered. We will become better parents, children, husbands, wives, employers, workers, neighbours and citizens. We will become better human beings. This transformation begins at our conversion and will not be completed until our glorification (Philippians 3:12–14).

As we experience this transforming work of God in our lives, let us consider the following:

- The goal set before us:
  1) to become like our God himself, with his image and likeness restored in us (Matthew 5:48; Ephesians 5:1; Colossians 3:10; 1 Peter 1:15–16)

2) to become like the Lord Jesus Christ (Romans 8:29; 13:14; Philippians 2:5; 1 Peter 2:21; 1 John 2:6)

3) to live in complete obedience to all of God's will as revealed in his Word (Psalm 119:28; Matthew 28:20; John 15:14; Colossians 1:9, 10; 1 John 5:3)

4) to cease from all sin (Psalm 119:133; John 8:11; 1 John 2:1)

**Psalm 119:133**
Direct my steps by Your word, And let no iniquity have dominion over me.

5) to love God, fellow believers, neighbours and enemies, recognizing that love is the fulfillment of the law and that without it we are nothing (Matthew 22:37–40; Luke 6:27; John 13:34–35; Romans 13:8–10; 1 Corinthians 13:1–8,13; Galatians 5:6; Colossians 3:14; 2 John 5–6)

**Luke 6:27**
"But I say to you who hear: Love your enemies, do good to those who hate you..."

- The opposition arrayed against us:
  1) this present evil world, with its ungodly philosophies and practices (Psalm 1:1; Romans 12:2; Colossians 2:8; James 4:4; 1 John 2:16)

**1 John 2:16**
For all that is in the world—the lust of the flesh, the lust of the eyes, and the pride of life—is not of the Father but is of the world.

  2) our own remaining sinful desires, which will fight against holiness until we die (Galatians 5:17; James 1:14; 4:1; 1 John 1:8)

  3) our adversary, the devil, and his demonic hosts of darkness (Job 2:4–5; Ephesians 6:11–12; 1 Peter 5:8; Revelation 12:17)

- The encouragements given to us:
  1) God the Father is committed to our transformation (John 15:1–2; Ephesians 2:10; Philippians 1:6; 2:12–13; 1 Thessalonians 5:23–24; Jude 24).

**Ephesians 2:10**
For we are His workmanship, created in Christ Jesus for good works, which God prepared beforehand that we should walk in them.

  2) Our union with Jesus Christ the Son makes a world of difference in the fight

against sin (Colossians 3:1–17; Romans 6:1–23). In Christ we are no longer in the flesh, under the law, slaves of sin, dead in Adam (Romans 5:17; 6:14,17–18; 7:4–6; 8:9). In Christ, we are dead to the reign of sin and alive to God (Romans 6:6–11; Colossians 3:1–3); and because Christ has completed the race of faith successfully, so shall we with his help (Hebrews 2:10–11,18; 4:14–16; 6:19–20; 12:1–2).

3) Every believer has the Holy Spirit as one of the greatest blessings of the new covenant (Ezekiel 36:27; 37:14; Acts 2:38; Galatians 3:14).[1] The Holy Spirit gives power to produce spiritual fruit and to put sin to death (Romans 8:13; Galatians 5:16,22–23); he gives understanding of the truth to all believers (John 15:26; 1 Corinthians 2:9–12; 1 John 2:20–21); and the Spirit is the means through which Christ gives gifts to the church that we might edify one another (1 Corinthians 12:7; Ephesians 4:11–16; 1 Peter 4:10).

• The responsibility resting upon us:
It is important to remember that our Saviour warned us, "without Me you can do nothing" (John 15:5). An attitude of humble, prayerful dependence must characterize our pursuit of holiness. It is also important to remember that strengthened by the Lord, it is we who must take responsibility for carrying out his commands. We are not to remain passive (2 Corinthians 7:1). We are exhorted to:

---

[1] See chapter 8 for more on the Holy Spirit and his work.

1) work out our own salvation with fear and trembling (Philippians 2:12)
2) discipline our bodies and bring them into subjection (1 Corinthians 9:27)
3) fight the good fight of faith (1 Timothy 6:12)
4) run the race set before us (Hebrews 12:1)
5) present our bodies a living sacrifice to God (Romans 12:1)
6) giving all diligence, add to our faith virtue, etc. (2 Peter 1:5–7)

1 Timothy 6:12
Fight the good fight of faith, lay hold on eternal life, to which you were also called and have confessed the good confession in the presence of many witnesses.

- The motivations working in us:
One of our greatest needs as believers is to fill our minds and hearts with what will move us the most to live holy lives (Philippians 4:8). These motivations are
1) the fear of the Lord, and being full of awe in his presence, which will cause us to walk carefully before him (Genesis 39:9; Nehemiah 5:15; Proverbs 1:7; 16:6; Acts 9:31; 2 Corinthians 7:1; 1 Peter 1:17)
2) love for Jesus Christ, for what will we not do for One whom we love so much? (Matthew 26:6–13; John 14:15; 2 Corinthians 5:14; 1 John 4:10–11)
3) gratitude for grace for such undeserved kindnesses which will produce a life of thanksgiving (Psalm 116:16–19; Romans 12:1; 2 Corinthians 8:7,9; 9:15)
4) faith in a glorious future—the promise of good things to come—which will make us seek to daily live in joyful obedience (Hebrews 11:24–26; 2 Peter 3:14; 1 John 3:3)

Romans 12:1
I beseech you therefore, brethren, by the mercies of God, that you present your bodies a living sacrifice, holy, acceptable to God, which is your reasonable service.

- The spiritual disciplines required of us:

Some personal or individual disciplines:

1) profiting from the Word of God (Psalm 1:2–3; 119:11; 2 Timothy 3:16; 1 Peter 2:2)
2) communing with God in prayer (Isaiah 40:31; Mark 14:38; Ephesians 6:18; 1 Thessalonians 5:17; Jude 20–21)
3) benefiting from and growing through trials and suffering (Psalm 119:67,71; Romans 5:3–4; Hebrews 2:10; 5:8; 12:9–11; James 1:2–4; 1 Peter 1:6–7)
4) maintaining a good conscience (Acts 24:16; 1 Timothy 1:5,19; 3:9; 1 Peter 3:16)

Some public or corporate disciplines:

1) hearing the preaching and teaching of the Word of God (2 Timothy 4:2–4)
2) fellowshipping together by engaging in Christ-centred worship, exhortation, sharing and service (1 Thessalonians 5:14; 1 Peter 2:5)
3) observing the Lord's Supper (1 Corinthians 10:16, 17; 11:23–26)
4) meeting together for prayer (Matthew 18:20; Acts 4:23–31; 2 Thessalonians 3:1–2)

Above and beyond everything else, our growth in present sanctification will be directly proportionate to our concentration on Jesus Christ. The more we look to him and seek to know him and the power of his resurrection and the fellowship of his sufferings, the more like him we will become (2 Corinthians 3:18; Philippians 3:8–10; Hebrews 12:2; 2 Peter 3:18).

**Romans 5:3–4**
And not only *that*, but we also glory in tribulations, knowing that tribulation produces perseverance; and perseverance, character; and character, hope.

## Sanctification—a future certainty

The blessed hope of every believer is the promised appearing of our great God and Saviour Jesus Christ (Titus 2:13; 1 John 3:2). It is by this glorious sight that God will complete that good work he has begun, to the praise of the glory of his grace! Then, with our spirits made perfect and our bodies made like Christ's resurrection body, we will be fully sanctified (Philippians 3:20–21; 1 Thessalonians 5:23).

**1 John 3:2**
Beloved, now we are children of God; and it has not yet been revealed what we shall be, but we know that when He is revealed, we shall be like Him, for we shall see Him as He is.

**1 Thessalonians 5:23**
Now may the God of peace Himself sanctify you completely; and may your whole spirit, soul, and body be preserved blameless at the coming of our Lord Jesus Christ.

To be saved is to be preserved in the faith to the end. "He that shall endure unto the end, the same shall be saved"(Matthew 24:13). Not that perseverance is an accident in Christianity, or a thing performed by human industry; they that are saved "are kept by the power of God, through faith unto salvation" (1 Peter 1:3–6). But perseverance is absolutely necessary to the complete saving of the soul....He that goeth to sea with a purpose to arrive at Spain, cannot arrive there if he be drowned by the way; wherefore perseverance is absolutely necessary to the saving of the soul.

*John Bunyan (1628–1688)*

# 11 The preservation and perseverance of the saints
Jim Elliff

God promises to hold every true believer securely until he delivers him to heaven, no matter what temptations or trials he encounters. Though the believer sins, he will not finally fail, but will be kept by God's power through the gift of persevering faith. This doctrine is called the preservation and perseverance of the saints. We will take a look at each side of this great doctrine. Here is a simple way to think of it: God will *preserve* every true believer, but he will not do so without *persevering* faith, a faith he alone gives (1 Peter 1:5–7).

## The preservation of the saints
God keeps hold of believers with a five-finger grip (2 Timothy 1:12b):

1) We are kept by the *promise* of God (John 6:37–39).
2) We are kept by the *power* of God (John 10:28–30).
3) We are kept by the *passion* of God (Romans 8:38–39).
4) We are kept by the *priesthood* of God (Hebrews 7:23–25).

**1 Peter 1:5–7**
...who are kept by the power of God through faith for salvation ready to be revealed in the last time. In this you greatly rejoice, though now for a little while, if need be, you have been grieved by various trials, that the genuineness of your faith, *being* much more precious than gold that perishes, though it is tested by fire, may be found to praise, honor, and glory at the revelation of Jesus Christ...

**2 Timothy 1:12b**
...for I know whom I have believed and am persuaded that He is able to keep what I have committed to Him until that Day.

5) We are kept by the *presence* of God (Ephesians 1:13–14).

## The perseverance of the saints
The believer will never finally fail because God will make him persevere until the end. He will persevere in his faith, and in the fruit of that faith, good works.

**1 Peter 1:5,9**
...who are kept by the power of God through faith for salvation ready to be revealed in the last time....receiving the end of your faith—the salvation of *your* souls.

- The believer will persevere in his faith.
  God has made every Christian a life-long believer, that is, he will *continue* to trust God until the end (1 Peter 1:5,9).
  1) This faith is a gift from God (Ephesians 2:8–9).
  2) This faith can be examined and tested for durability and permanence (1 Peter 1:6–7; Colossians 1:21–23; Hebrews 3:5–6; Luke 8:13).
  Do you have a persevering faith or only a temporary faith? The faith God gives is persevering.

**Luke 8:15**
"But the ones *that* fell on the good ground are those who, having heard the word with a noble and good heart, keep *it* and bear fruit with patience."

- The believer will persevere in his fruit.
  Read 1 John 3:13–14 and Luke 8:15.
  1) These works are a gift of God (Ephesians 2:10).
  2) Good works are the result of true faith (James 2:26).
  3) These works may be examined and tested for durability and permanence (2 Corinthians 12:20–21; 13:5: Matthew 12:33).
  Do you have good works in your life, or only an outward show of religion? Are you continuing in good works?

## Conclusion

If you are a true believer you are safe forever in Christ (John 6:47; Hebrews 13:5b)!

If you profess to know Christ and yet do not have persevering faith and corresponding works, you have no real faith at all. Note the "if" in these verses that follow. The believer is truly saved only "if" he has true persevering faith in the first place (1 Corinthians 15:2; Colossians 1:22–23; Hebrews 3:12,14).

It is necessary, therefore, for you to continue in faith and corresponding works until the day you die. If you desire to do so and can do so, you are exhibiting true persevering faith—the faith that only God can give (Hebrews 12:1–2; Galatians 6:7–9; 1 Peter 1: 5–11; Jude 24–25).

**John 6:47**
"Most assuredly, I say to you, he who believes in Me has everlasting life."

**Jude 24–25**
Now to Him who is able to keep you from stumbling, And to present *you* faultless Before the presence of His glory with exceeding joy, To God our Savior, Who alone is wise, *Be* glory and majesty, Dominion and power, Both now and forever. Amen.

Before Christ comes I do not expect to see a perfect Church. There cannot be such a thing. The wheat and the chaff, in the present state of things, will always be found together. I pity those who leave one Church and join another, because of a few faults and unsound members. ...if men are too scrupulous, they may go fluttering about like Noah's dove all their days and never find rest.

*J.C. Ryle (1816–1900)*

# 12 The church
David Aspinall

The glory of Christ, while the Son of God was on earth, shone brightly without need of reflection. "We beheld his glory" John says (John 1:14). And when Christ comes again he will not need recourse to human testimony: "they will see the Son of Man coming on the clouds of heaven with power and great glory" (Matthew 24:30). But until that day the glory of Christ is veiled by heaven and by earth's blindness. Until then it is the privilege of believers, those who make up Christ's church, to make known the glory of Christ to the world. We have not beheld his glory, as the Apostles did, but we have the awesome responsibility of bearing witness to the Apostles' testimony of Christ's glory (John 17:19–21).

As God the Father was glorified in Christ Jesus, so now do the Father and Christ seek to be glorified in the church (Ephesians 3:21; John 17:4,10,22). We who believe constitute "the church of God which He purchased with His own blood" (Acts 20:28), or, as this passage may also be rendered, "with the blood of His own [Son]." Having been purchased by God, we are both his servants and his sons. Although we cannot forfeit our inheritance as the sons of God, we can fail to

**John 1:14**
And the Word became flesh and dwelt among us, and we beheld His glory, the glory as of the only begotten of the Father, full of grace and truth.

**Ephesians 3:21**
...to Him be glory in the church by Christ Jesus to all generations forever and ever. Amen.

glorify him, and therefore forfeit many of the great privileges that would be otherwise ours as faithful children (Matthew 25:14–30; 1 Corinthians 3:12–15).

John 16:14
"He will glorify Me, for He will take of what is Mine and declare *it* to you."

The Holy Spirit, who indwells the believer, has the task of glorifying Christ in the present age (John 16:14). If we who make up the church fail to glorify Christ, we therefore grieve the Holy Spirit (Ephesians 4:30). The unalterable fact of our salvation must never make us forget that we are *saved in order to serve* Christ and his body, the church. Rather, the magnificence of our calling and destiny should excite in us the desire to exercise all the privileges of our sonship now (1 Corinthians 6:20).

1 Corinthians 6:20
For you were bought at a price; therefore glorify God in your body and in your spirit, which are God's.

### A church without knowledge of truth cannot glorify Christ

The church, says the Apostle Paul, is "the pillar and ground of the truth" (1 Timothy 3:15).

In the church, emphasis should be given to carrying out the great commandment, "You shall love the LORD your God with all your heart, and with all your soul, and *with all your mind*" (Matthew 22:37; see also Deuteronomy 6:5). We have deliberately stressed the last phrase because there are those in the church who would separate the intellectual life from the devotional life of faith, love, patience and good works. Christ does not separate "heart and soul" Christianity from the exertion of the mind and intellect. Neither does Paul, who prays that the churches under his care "be filled with the knowledge of His will in all wisdom and spiritual understanding; that you may walk worthy of the Lord, fully pleasing *Him*, being fruitful in every good work and increasing in the knowledge of God" (Colossians 1:9–10). Paul does not view knowledge as an end unto itself, which leads to pride (1 Corinthians 8:1b), but as the indispensable handmaiden to purity and an obedient life (Ephesians 1:15–19; Philippians 1:9–11). After all, how can we serve a Master whose will we have not consulted? Or expect a reward from the Lord whose commands we have neglected (Matthew 24:45–51; Luke 17:7–10)?

It is particularly the task of the pastors and teachers in the church to place before the sheep under their care "the whole counsel [or, purpose] of God" (Acts 20:27). Paul considered that this faithful discharge of his call as a shepherd rendered him "innocent of the blood of all *men*," (Acts 20:26) and he went on to urge the Ephesian elders: "Therefore take heed to yourselves and to all the flock, among which the Holy Spirit has made you overseers, to shepherd the church of God which He purchased with His own blood" (Acts 20:28). Those who are called as pastors and teachers, therefore, cannot afford to neglect *any* part of the divine revelation which the Lord has given the church (2 Timothy 3:16).

Paul exalts the office of pastor and teacher. In the Apostle's view, these callings are vital for the life of the church (Ephesians 4:8,11–13). Without the shepherding care of leaders such

**1 Corinthians 8:1b**
...Knowledge puffs up, but love edifies.

**2 Timothy 3:16**
All Scripture is given by inspiration of God, and *is* profitable for doctrine, for reproof, for correction, for instruction in righteousness...

**Ephesians 4:8,11–13**
Therefore He says: *"When He* [that is Christ] *ascended on high, He led captivity captive, And gave gifts to men."* ...And He Himself gave some to *be* apostles, some prophets, some evangelists, and some pastors and teachers, for the equipping of the saints for the work of ministry, for the edifying of the body of Christ, till we all come to the unity of the faith and of the knowledge of the Son of God, to a perfect man, to the measure of the stature of the fullness of Christ.

as pastors and teachers, who to build rightly must build upon the foundational work of the Apostles and prophets as found in Scripture (Ephesians 2:20), we cannot expect to achieve unity, knowledge of the Son of God or the maturity which that knowledge should engender in us.

Paul goes on to describe further dangers we will avoid by recognizing the various gifts he has given the church (Ephesians 4:14). Without acknowledgement of Christ's pastors and teachers, therefore, we will remain immature, subject to the danger of deception by those savage wolves who, as Paul had warned the Ephesian elders before, would draw away disciples after themselves (Acts 20:29–30). There cannot be unity, stability or growth in the church—growth in *maturity*, that is, *not* numbers—where Christ's gifts in men are neglected.

**Ephesians 4:14**
...that we should no longer be children, tossed to and fro and carried about with every wind of doctrine, by the trickery of men, in the cunning craftiness of deceitful plotting...

### A church without holiness cannot glorify Christ

The church is anointed by "the Spirit of truth" (John 16:13; 1 John 2:27). But the Spirit of truth which indwells the church is more often called the *Holy* Spirit. That fact alone should warn believers as to the seriousness with which we should take the admonition, "You shall be holy, for I the LORD your God *am* holy" (Leviticus 19:2b). Knowledge and truth are not, as we said before, an end to themselves. They serve, rather, to render the church more fit for its work.

What is the destiny of the church? Those

who make up the church of Jesus Christ are saints, as well as sons and servants of God. "Saint" means "holy one." Christians are holy because of their standing in Christ (justification), but as well they are in the process of being made holy by the Spirit (sanctification). Israel was given the unique privilege of revelation from God, that she might be a holy nation (Exodus 19:5–6; Amos 3:2; Psalm 147:19–20; Romans 3:1–2). Likewise the church, Paul says in Ephesians, has been chosen "in Him [that is, Christ] before the foundation of the world, that we should be *holy and without blame* before him [italics mine]." Let us note that Paul mentions this election to holiness *before* he adds, "in love, having predestined us to adoption as sons by Jesus Christ to Himself" (Ephesians 1:4,5a). All this, the Apostle writes, is "to the praise of the glory of His grace" (Ephesians 1:6).

The Spirit, John assures us, is not given merely to instruct the church, but to convict and comfort her as well (John 16:7–15). Conviction of sin *must* come before the comfort of mercy, just as the law came before the gospel. Only by the Spirit of truth working with our minds, hearts and consciences can we come to "the measure of the stature of the fullness of Christ" (Ephesians 4:13b). The Holy Spirit has the task of sanctifying us completely, for holiness and sanctification are qualities "without which no one will see the Lord" (Hebrews 12:14b).

It is also by the work of the Spirit that we can bring forth the fruit of the Spirit

**Galatians 5:22–23**
But the fruit of the Spirit is love, joy, peace, longsuffering, kindness, goodness, faithfulness, gentleness, self-control. Against such there is no law.

(Galatians 5:22–23), by which qualities, as much as by our words, the world will recognize Christ in us. A church which walks after the flesh rather than by the Spirit cannot glorify Christ, for "the flesh sets its desire against the Spirit" (Galatians 5:17; see also verse 16). In Romans 12 there is yet again a connection between wholeness of heart and soundness of mind. See Paul's admonition to believers in Romans 12:1–2. Paul will not compromise with those who suggest we can be fruitful, even more 'spiritual' Christians *without* loving God with our whole mind as well as heart and soul. The sacrifice that God accepts on his holy altar, Paul knows, is the *whole* believer, nothing less.

## A church without love cannot glorify Christ

It is providential that the Apostle Paul, while writing to the church in Corinth, about which we know far more that is negative than positive, should address the members of that congregation in terms unmistakeably endearing. Despite their immorality, he calls the Corinthians saints (1 Corinthians 1:2); in spite of their disunity, he calls them brethren (1 Corinthians 2:1; 3:1); and in spite of their lack of love, he calls them beloved (1 Corinthians 15:58). In fact, it is in this very letter to the Corinthians, chapter 13, that Paul includes his "hymn to love"—not in praise of the Corinthians' display of Christian love but in deploring their lack of love to one another. Despite this, Paul still regards the Corinthian church as his beloved

**1 Corinthians 1:2**
To the church of God which is at Corinth, to those who are sanctified in Christ Jesus, called *to be* saints, with all who in every place call on the name of Jesus Christ our Lord, both theirs and ours.

children (1 Corinthians 4:14).

We must see the long-standing disunity and lack of love among genuine Christians as the scandal it is. How the Lord's heart must grieve over lack of love among Christians. We must not forget that the two great commandments have to do with love, love first to God, then, like unto it, love to one another (Matthew 22:37–39). The Apostle John will not countenance a Christian claim which fails this crucial test (1 John 4:20).

How, though, can we love brethren with whom we refuse to fellowship? Sectarianism is the death of love. For we cannot love our brethren, according to John, from a safe distance (1 John 3:16–18). Christ did not 'love' from afar and neither can we (2 Thessalonians 3:14–15). *Do we love the brotherhood?*

The church, built on the apostolic confession that Jesus of Nazareth is the Christ, the Son of God, is still the object of his husbandly devotion (Matthew 16:18). Even when those who gather in his name are very few, he is there among them (Matthew 18:20). The Lord is indeed the Judge before whom all will ultimately stand. But he is also the Good Shepherd, who seeks the stray. Let us remember the Lord's loyal under-shepherd Peter, a shepherd who once strayed himself, who one night heard the Chief Shepherd heal his own backsliding with the admonition "When you have returned to *Me*, strengthen your brethren" (Luke 22:32). Hearing Peter, let us make it our goal, as those who have also tasted the grace of Christ, to love the brotherhood

**1 John 4:20**
If someone says, "I love God," and hates his brother, he is a liar; for he who does not love his brother whom he has seen, how can he love God whom he has not seen?

**1 John 3:16–18**
By this we know love, because He laid down His life for us. And we also ought to lay down *our* lives for the brethren. But whoever has this world's goods, and sees his brother in need, and shuts up his heart from him, how does the love of God abide in him? My little children, let us not love in word or in tongue, but in deed and in truth.

**1 Peter 2:17**
Honor all *people*. Love
the brotherhood. Fear
God. Honor the king.

(1 Peter 2:17). Particularly because it is made up of clay vessels, spared only by grace, the church is peculiarly fitted to bear the gospel of grace, that which sets Christianity apart from all other faiths. Grace, we might add, must be not only the centre of our message to the world but also the cement of our fellowship in the church.

Worship is ultimate, …because God is ultimate, not man.

*John Piper (1946– )*

# 13 Worship
Michael A.G. Haykin

Christian worship—what it entails and how it should be done—is one of the most controversial issues of our day. "Should we use hymnal or songbook or simply sing from an overhead projector?" "Should we sit in pews or folding chairs?" "What style of music should we use?" "What kind of instruments should we play?" "What kind of preaching is appropriate?" "How should we pray—with written prayers? Raising our hands?"[1] It is increasingly evident that evangelicals are deeply divided over the answers to these questions and others that relate to worship.

In such a situation it is vital to begin with basics. Answering these questions must not be our first priority. We must first lay out the basics of worship.

## Worship is first and foremost about God
The first question of *The Westminster Shorter Catechism* (1648) helps set the stage for our thinking about worship. The first question of the catechism asks: "What is the chief end of man?" And the answer: "To glorify God and enjoy him for ever." The goal of worship, like the rest of life, is to glorify God: to joyfully declare his primacy and sovereignty in all

[1] For these questions, see Robert Godfrey, *Pleasing God in our Worship* (Wheaton, Illinois: Crossway Books, 1999), 10.

things, to set forth with delight his excellence and the perfection of his character, and to adore him for all that he has done, is doing, and will do for us in creation and redemption. In other words, worship is first and foremost about God—not about us and our personal likes and dislikes with regard to styles of music, for example, or whether or not we feel good about our experience of worship. If God is not glorified and honoured in our worship, then worship is not taking place (Psalm 96:8).

### Worship—God-centred

An excellent example of such God-centred worship is found in the adoration of God by the four living creatures in heaven, as recorded in Revelation 4:8b: "Holy, holy, holy, Lord God Almighty, who was and is and is to come!" Two questions then need to be raised:

1) What does this verse tell us about God-centred worship?

    It involves the adoration of the character of God.

2) What three attributes of God are praised here?

    • God is worshiped here as the Holy One, the One who is utterly unique in the universe and who possesses absolute moral purity.

    • The four living creatures acknowledge God's sovereignty, for they refer to him as the "Lord God Almighty." This statement underscores God's omnipotence and rule over all things, his unrivaled power and supremacy over the entire universe.

- God is worshipped by the four living creatures as eternal. They declare him to be the One "who was and is and is to come." These designations emphasize God's self-existence and eternity. The four heavenly creatures thus worship God for who he is, namely, the eternally existent and present One.

Of the various aspects of our worship we must then ask: How are these God-centred? Do they reveal God's glorious character and attributes or do they obscure them? Do they affirm his uniqueness and moral excellence, his utter sovereignty and eternity? And do they help bring men and women and children to the place where they delight in glorifying God?

### Worship—focused on the Lord Jesus Christ

There is one thing above all other things that we know brings glory to God and delights his heart. What is that? The worship of his unique Son, the Lord Jesus Christ. Consider, for instance, the following verses: John 5:22–23; John 12:26; John 14:13; John 17:5 (especially note the request "glorify Me together with Yourself"); John 16:13–14. This last text records important words that Jesus spoke to his disciples on the night of his betrayal.

John 16:13–14
"However, when He, the Spirit of truth, has come, He will guide you into all truth; for He will not speak on His own *authority*, but whatever He hears He will speak; and He will tell you things to come. He will glorify Me, for He will take of what is Mine and declare *it* to you."

Here, in the words "He will glorify Me," we have set forth for us what has been rightly called the distinctive role of the Holy Spirit in the New Covenant. He has come to turn the attention of men and women away from themselves and even away from himself and focus their eyes on Christ. The Holy Spirit has come into our lives in order that we should focus our thoughts and affections on Christ; that we should live lives that bring honour to the name of Jesus; that we should love Christ and adore him.

And this is especially true of worship. The Holy Spirit has come to make our worship Christ-centred. And note, this is God the Father's design and delight, for he has sent the Spirit for this very purpose (John 14:26). Genuine worship has this one indispensable mark—it focuses on Christ. For a picture of such Christ-centred worship, see Revelation 5.

Here, then, is a second rule by which all worship must be measured: Is it Christ-centred?

## A new way of worship

Not only is the Lord Jesus the focus of New Testament worship, he is also its legislator and mediator (John 4:20–24). The encounter of Jesus with the Samaritan woman raises the following four points which are relevant to our discussion:

1) The Samaritan woman's interest is focused on the *place* of worship (verse 20).

**John 4:20–24**
"Our fathers worshiped on this mountain, and you *Jews* say that in Jerusalem is the place where one ought to worship." Jesus said to her, "Woman, believe Me, the hour is coming when you will neither on this mountain, nor in Jerusalem, worship the Father. You worship what you do not know; we know what we worship, for salvation is of the Jews. But the hour is coming, and now is, when the true worshipers will worship the Father in spirit and truth; for the Father is seeking such to worship Him. God *is* Spirit, and those who worship Him must worship in spirit and truth."

2) Jesus shifts the discussion instead to the nature of *true* worship. Old Testament worship was commanded and mandated by God, to be sure (verse 22b); but nevertheless, as Jesus says, it clearly was to be superseded (verse 23). Jesus' ministry begins a new way of relating to God (compare with verse 21). Henceforth, true worship will be "in spirit and truth" (verse 24).

3) The meaning of the expression "in spirit and in truth" has been variously understood. One persuasive way of thinking about it is that it suggests that henceforth true worship, God-honouring worship, is through Christ. He is, after all, the truth (John 14:6), and he is the giver of the Spirit (John 7:37–39). In other words, Jesus, and he alone, is "the place" where true worship takes place. He is not only the object of worship, but he is the means by which true worship takes place.

4) This text is not contrasting inner reality with external form. God had always rejected the separation of these two (1 Samuel 15:22; Psalm 51:14–19; Isaiah 1:11–18). Forms are not wrong in themselves. Worship is never simply mental. An important question is then: What forms are to be present in Christian worship? In the New Covenant, all of the Old Testament forms of worship have been replaced by "a new and living way," in which Christ is the mediator of our worship.

## Trinitarian worship

Finally, our worship is trinitarian. Usually when we think of this, we put it this way: we worship God the Father *through* the Son *in the power* of the Holy Spirit (Philippians 3:3; Ephesians 2:18; 1 Corinthians 12:3).

**Ephesians 2:18**
For through Him [that is Christ] we both have access by one Spirit to the Father.

As our God-centred, Christ-focused worship is offered to the triune God may God help us to remember that it is for this that we have been created and it is this that we shall delight in throughout the eternal ages to come.

If Jesus Christ be God and died for me, no sacrifice can be too great for me to make for him.

C.T. Studd (1862–1931)

# 14 Missions

Peter Pikkert

A mission field is any community without a resident evangelical church to which the Holy Spirit can direct those in whom he is working. The mystery of missions occurs when godly missionaries enter such communities to stay. When they do, the Holy Spirit, prepares people from that community to receive the gospel message (Acts 10:44–45). The missionary's goal is to be used by the Holy Spirit in such communities to lead people to repentance of sin, faith in Jesus Christ and thus the receiving of forgiveness of sin and eternal life, to disciple new believers (that is, teach them sound doctrine so they will grow in grace), to baptize them and to integrate them into local church fellowships.

An unbiblical view of missions exposes the missionary enterprise to one of two risks. It can make the missionary task too small, under the excuse that there is enough work to be done at home, or by asserting that God, in his sovereign grace, will save the lost in his own time without our involvement.

Conversely, it can lead to attempts to "Christianize" the world. The missionary task is not to bring all men to Christ, but to proclaim Christ to all men (Romans 15:20).

**Acts 10:44–45**
While Peter was still speaking these words, the Holy Spirit fell upon all those who heard the word. And those of the circumcision who believed were astonished, as many as came with Peter, because the gift of the Holy Spirit had been poured out on the Gentiles also.

Clear goals and right motivation enables the church, the mission agency and the individual missionary to persevere in missions in difficult or seemingly fruitless situations as well as resist over-involvement in development and/or social work.

## God's justice does not demand missions

God's justice decreed that when man sinned he would suffer everlastingly (Genesis 2:16–17; 3:19; Jeremiah 31:30; Ezekiel 18:4; 33:8; Romans 5:17; Hebrews 9:27; Matthew 25:30,41,46; Mark 9:43,48). On the day of judgment no one will complain that God has treated him unjustly. We will, in fact, condemn ourselves. We not only fail to live up to God's law, we even fail by the standard we expect of others (Romans 2:1)! God has no "moral obligation" to save. Salvation—and thus missions—flows from his grace.

**Jeremiah 31:30**
"But every one shall die for his own iniquity; every man who eats the sour grapes, his teeth shall be set on edge."

## Mankind does not want missions

Mankind rejects the missionary message because it is blind concerning the gospel of salvation (Romans 3:9–18; 2 Corinthians 4:3–4; Ephesians 4:18), under the power of darkness and energized by Satan (Colossians 1:13; Ephesians 2:1–2; 1 John 5:19). As long as missionaries make educational, medical or developmental contributions they may be tolerated; but when they concentrate on evangelism, discipling and church planting, they are often reviled. This is expected, for they are stepping into enemy territory.

**1 John 5:19**
We know that we are of God, and the whole world lies *under the sway of* the wicked one.

## Scriptural authority for missions

Throughout the Scriptures, there is a clear missionary emphasis:

- In the character of God
  The Bible uses the concept of light to describe God (John 1:5–9; 1 John 1:5; 2:8–10). Just as light is diffusive, enlivening, enlightening, penetrating darkness, so God, in his grace, seeks to penetrate spiritually dark places to destroy the works of the wicked one (1 John 3:8) and to introduce spiritual light, life and goodness (John 8:12). Furthermore, God's love motivates him to communicate with the objects of his favour. His love is outgoing, sacrificial and comprehensive, encompassing the world (John 3:16). He is a God of relationships.

  **1 John 1:5**
  This is the message which we have heard from Him and declare to you, that God is light and in Him is no darkness at all.

- In election
  1) In the Old Testament, God chose a man, Abraham, and his descendants, the Jewish people, to make them channels of blessing to the whole world (Genesis 12:3b; 18:18; 22:17–18; 26:2–4; 28:12–14).

  **Genesis 12:3b**
  "...in you all the families of the earth shall be blessed."

  2) God chose Israel so that it would serve him as a nation of priests and prophets to minister to the other nations (Exodus 19:5–6). The tragedy of the Old Testament is that the Jews failed to discern God's purpose for them, and so God set them aside as a failure.

  **Exodus 19:5–6**
  "'Now therefore, if you will indeed obey My voice and keep My covenant, then you shall be a special treasure to Me above all people; for all the earth is Mine. And you shall be to Me a kingdom of priests and a holy nation.' These are the words which you shall speak to the children of Israel."

  3) The doctrine of election as expounded in the New Testament is meant to be both an encouragement for evangelism

(Acts 18:9) and an assurance that God will use his people for eternal purposes (2 Timothy 2:10; Ephesians 1:11–12).

- In the Old Testament

  1) In spite of Israel's failure, we still catch numerous glimpses of God's concern for the nations through such people as Joseph, Jethro, Rahab, the widow of Zarephath, Naaman, Jonah and Daniel.

  2) Solomon grasped something of God's purpose for Israel when he prayed (1 Kings 8:41–43).

  3) The Psalms are full of the universal implications of God's rule. Up to one third of the Psalms address the Gentiles positively (Psalm 67:1–2; 72:8,17,19; 87:4; see also Psalm 2, 22, 47, 50, 96).

  4) The prophets had a worldwide vision, even when their main message pertained to Israel (Isaiah 45:22; 52:10; Jeremiah 1:5; Malachi 1:11). Daniel's witness was so effective that two heathen kings proclaimed Jehovah to be the most high God, whose kingdom was everlasting and universal (Daniel 2:47; 3:28–29; 4:34–37; 6:26–27).

  5) Esther, Ezekiel, Ruth, Obadiah, Nahum all contain interaction with Gentiles, and in Job, Proverbs, Ecclesiastes and The Song of Solomon the interaction is generic. In short, we can trace God's concern for the whole earth in every part of the Old Testament.

- In the New Testament

  1) The Gospels give us the life-story of Jesus,

God's great missionary. His lineage contains a number of Gentile women, Tamar, Rahab and Ruth. The angels heralded his birth as "good tidings of great joy which will be to all people" (Luke 2:10). Simeon proclaimed him to be "a light to *bring* revelation to the Gentiles" (Luke 2:32), and John the Baptist described him as "the Lamb of God who takes away the sin of the world!" (John 1:29). Although Jesus' personal ministry was to "the lost sheep of Israel," his thoughts, aims and teachings were global (Matthew 8:11; 13:38a; John 3:16; 8:12; 9:5b; 10:16).

2) Jesus reminded his hometown that God chose a Gentile widow to feed Elijah and healed Naaman. His miracles and parables encompassed Gentiles: a Roman centurion, a Syro-phoenician woman and a Samaritan. All four Gospels culminate in Jesus' great commission commands, which envision the evangelization of the whole world by God's people (Mattthew 28:18–20; Mark 16:15; Luke 24:47; John 20:21).

3) The Acts of the Apostles is the inspired record of missionary work during the first century. Acts 1:8 serves as the book's contents page: "But you shall receive power when the Holy Spirit has come upon you; and you shall be witnesses to Me in Jerusalem, and in all Judea and Samaria, and to the end of the earth." Acts chapters 2 to 7 tells the story of the disciples'

**Matthew 13:38a**
The field is the world…

**John 3:16**
"For God so loved the world that He gave His only begotten Son, that whoever believes in Him should not perish but have everlasting life."

**John 8:12**
Then Jesus spoke to them again, saying, "I am the light of the world. He who follows Me shall not walk in darkness, but have the light of life."

**John 9:5b**
"…I am the light of the world."

**Mark 16:15**
And He said to them, "Go into all the world and preach the gospel to every creature."

witness in Jerusalem, and chapters 8 to 12 give glimpses of outreach to Judea and Samaria respectively, along with Paul's conversion. From chapter 13 on, the narrative follows Paul and his fellow workers as they take the gospel "to the ends of the earth." Acts ends abruptly with Paul at Rome, where he was "preaching the kingdom of God and teaching the things which concern the Lord Jesus Christ with all confidence, no one forbidding him" (Acts 28:31). This is appropriate, for the work of missions was to continue.

4) The epistles are missionary letters sent to new churches, new converts and the next generation of missionaries. They deal with practical, doctrinal and other matters facing new believers in hostile Judaic or pagan societies, and urge them to engage in missions (Romans 10:14–15).

5) Revelation was written by a banished missionary to comfort and encourage new Christians persecuted by a government seeking to destroy the remarkable results of the early church's missionary work. The book describes the final phases of the missionary era: the further growth of the church, the vindication of the people of God, the overthrow of all authorities in opposition to God and the establishment of God's universal kingdom of righteousness (Revelation 5:9; 11:15).

**Revelation 5:9**
And they sang a new song, saying: "You are worthy to take the scroll, And to open its seals; For You were slain, And have redeemed us to God by Your blood Out of every tribe and tongue and people and nation..."

**Revelation 11:15**
Then the seventh angel sounded: And there were loud voices in heaven, saying, "The kingdoms of this world have become *the kingdoms* of our Lord and of His Christ, and He shall reign forever and ever!"

**Conclusion**

The Bible is a thoroughly missionary book. Those who accept it as their sole rule of faith must be committed to worldwide missions. Missions is, in fact, central in the church's duties and responsibilities in the world.

It seems, then, we are forced to believe in a real Right and Wrong. People may be sometimes mistaken about them, just as people sometimes get their sums wrong; but they are not a matter of mere taste and opinion any more than the multiplication table. Now if we are agreed about that, I go on to my next point, which is this. None of us are really keeping the Law of Nature.... I hope you will not misunderstand what I am going to say. I am not preaching, and heaven knows I do not pretend to be better than anyone else. I am only trying to call attention to a fact; the fact that this year, or this month, or, more likely, this very day, we have failed to practice ourselves the kind of behaviour we expect from other people.

*C.S. Lewis (1898–1963)*

# 15 Christian ethics
David B. Morris

The Holy Scriptures are the Word of God, who has communicated his mind and will to man. Thus, the Scriptures provide the foundation for ethics and its authority. The subject of ethics addresses human conduct, the standard of that conduct and moral judgment. Genuinely Christian ethics must be rooted in the authoritative Word of God.

## The foundation of Christian ethics

The question of human identity is foundational to questions about conduct raised by ethics. That is, "Who am I?" must be addressed before dealing with "How should I behave?" God has answered this most important question that informs all of life. In the account of creation we read of the uniqueness of humanity among all that God made (Genesis 1:26–27).

In contrast to vegetation and animals, which were made "according to its kind" (Genesis 1:11–12,21,24,25), humanity was created in God's image. Moses declared the character of the God in whose image man was made: "He is the Rock, His work *is* perfect; For all His ways *are* justice, a God of truth and without injustice; Righteous and upright is He" (Deuteronomy 32:4).

**Genesis 1:26–27**
Then God said, "Let Us make man in Our image, according to Our likeness; let them have dominion over the fish of the sea, over the birds of the air, and over the cattle, over all the earth and over every creeping thing that creeps on the earth." So God created man in His *own* image; in the image of God He created him; male and female He created them.

Man was made to reflect morally this righteous character of God as his image-bearer. As the crown of God's creation, man is to reflect the glory of God. Thus, all of human life is to be directed toward the goal of mirroring the excellence of God's person. This truth provides the premise for human accountability and ethical behaviour. This accountability is seen in the command which God gave man to obey in the Garden of Eden (Genesis 2:16–17).

### The summary of ethical duty

Because man has been created in God's image, he is responsible to obey God. Man has a moral duty to his Maker. In both the Old and New Testaments this duty is summarized as supreme love to God coupled with love to others who bear God's image. Our Lord Jesus expressed this in the Gospel of Matthew in response to a question by a scribe (Matthew 22:36–40). Jesus quotes from Israel's confession of faith in Deuteronomy 6:4–5 and the words of Leviticus 19:18 in answering the scribe's question. These commands form the basis of every other moral responsibility to God and man. Paul states this same summary of our duty to one another in his letter to the Romans (Romans 13:8–11).

Interestingly, both these commands are relational in nature. They address our duty to God and man in terms of relationship with others. This relational aspect of morality informs many biblical commands and underscores the realities of personhood and fellowship that mark the Scriptures.

When our Lord Jesus took to himself human personality without sin, he fulfilled these two great commandments of the Law to the Father's good pleasure (Matthew 3:17; John 8:29) as he loved God with all his being and his neighbour as himself.

**Matthew 3:17**
And suddenly a voice *came* from heaven, saying, "This is My beloved Son, in whom I am well pleased."

### The content of ethical duty

The summary of moral responsibility given in the command to love is filled out in definite commands found in both covenants. In his redemptive activity with Israel and his Church, God sets forth a demand for behaviour that reflects the privilege of being his people.

After the great events of the Exodus, God entered into covenant with Israel at Sinai. That covenant contained many moral stipulations that Israel was to obey. Among these, the Ten Commandments specified duties to God and one another. They also provide a helpful framework for integrating the various commands of the Law of Moses. The Law (Hebrew, *torah*: instruction) addressed human life in its many areas. Life at home, at court, in the marketplace, on the battlefield and at worship was morally governed for Israel by the Law. The ethical intent of the Law was brought into focus by Micah, the prophet, in Micah 6:8.

In his Letter to the Romans, Paul briefly addresses the issue of ethical conduct for the nations who did not possess the Law of Moses. He asserts that conscience reflects the

**Micah 6:8**
He has shown you, O man, what *is* good; And what does the LORD require of you But to do justly, To love mercy, And to walk humbly with your God?

**Romans 2:14–15**
(...for when Gentiles, who do not have the law, by nature do the things in the law, these, although not having the law, are a law to themselves, who show the work of the law written in their hearts, their conscience also bearing witness, and between themselves *their* thoughts accusing or else excusing *them*).

moral character of God, in whose image all people have been made. Read Romans 2:14–15. Thus, Paul says, conscience provides a standard of moral discrimination for those who were not possessors of God's special revelation in Scripture. This standard, in contrast to Scripture, is neither infallible nor saving.

The New Covenant Scriptures present the standard of conduct for the Christian church. Building on the Old Covenant Scriptures, our Lord Jesus and his Apostles have given to his church a canon, an inspired and authoritative body of writings, which inform the believer of the life he is called to lead in the world. Paul writes to the saints in Rome, "But God be thanked that *though* you were slaves of sin, yet you obeyed from the heart that form of doctrine to which you were delivered" (Romans 6:17). This "form of doctrine" by the grace of God produces "obedience to the faith among all nations" (Romans 1:5; 16:26). This moral obedience which gospel salvation produces stands in contrast to the believer's past, because he has been raised to "walk in newness of life"(Romans 6:4).

**Ephesians 4:20–24**
But you have not so learned Christ, if indeed you have heard Him and have been taught by Him, as the truth is in Jesus: that you put off, concerning your former conduct, the old man which grows corrupt according to the deceitful lusts, and be renewed in the spirit of your mind, and that you put on the new man which was created according to God, in true righteousness and holiness.

This moral obedience also stands in contrast to the lifestyle of the nations. Paul writes of this contrast in his letter to the Ephesians (Ephesians 4:20–24). This definitive break with the old life has occurred as believers have been taken out of union with Adam and placed in union with Jesus Christ. The result of this "new man," or redeemed humanity, is a life that reflects God's righteousness and holiness.

The believer's conduct is to evidence this righteousness in thought, word, deed and attitude. Our Lord Jesus presented this demand clearly in the Sermon on the Mount (Matthew 5–7). The Apostles also call for godly behaviour. Their letters contain imperatives that govern all of life. Responsibilities of marriage and singleness, family, work, citizenship and community are very practically addressed. The goal of all these commands, as in the whole of Scripture, is seen in 2 Timothy 3:17 (see also 2 Corinthians 3:18; Hebrews 13:20–21).

**2 Timothy 3:17**
...that the man of God may be complete, thoroughly equipped for every good work.

**Hebrews 13:20–21**
Now may the God of peace who brought up our Lord Jesus from the dead, that great Shepherd of the sheep, through the blood of the everlasting covenant, make you complete in every good work to do His will, working in you what is well pleasing in His sight, through Jesus Christ, to whom *be* glory forever and ever. Amen.

O Lord Jesus, how long, how long
'Ere we shout the glad song,
Christ returneth! Hallelujah!
Hallelujah! Amen, Hallelujah! Amen.

*H.L. Turner*

# 16 The second coming and the last judgment
Keith M. Edwards

The departure of Jesus from the earth recorded in Acts 1 was accompanied by a remarkable promise made through angelic messengers: "This *same* Jesus, who was taken up from you into heaven, will so come in like manner as you saw Him go into heaven" (Acts 1:11b).

Jesus Christ who was virgin born, lived among us, was crucified and rose again on the third day will one day return to the earth. Sadly the wonderful doctrine of Christ's second coming has generated much division within the body of Christ.

Two extremes should be avoided as we comes to the study of last things (eschatology). On the one hand, preoccupation and endless prophetic speculation does not harmonize with proclaiming "the whole counsel of God." In contrast, many avoid the issue to skirt a controversial and difficult subject over which many fine scholars differ.

## Correctives concerning Christ's return

No one knows the day nor hour when the Lord is coming again (Matthew 24:42; 25:13; 2 Peter 3:10). Throughout church history many individuals and groups have erred by claiming "special insight" into the timing of Christ's coming. Their error and foolish

**Matthew 24:42**
"Watch therefore, for you do not know what hour your Lord is coming."

**2 Peter 3:10**
But the day of the Lord will come as a thief in the night, in which the heavens will pass away with a great noise, and the elements will melt with fervent heat; both the earth and the works that are in it will be burned up.

**1 John 3:3**
And everyone who has this hope in Him purifies himself, just as He is pure.

**2 Peter 3:11**
...what manner *of persons* ought you to be in holy conduct and godliness...

**Titus 2:12–13**
...we should live soberly, righteously, and godly in the present age, looking for the blessed hope and glorious appearing of our great God and Savior Jesus Christ...

**Matthew 24:30**
"Then the sign of the Son of Man will appear in heaven, and then all the tribes of the earth will mourn, and they will see the Son of Man coming on the clouds of heaven with power and great glory."

**Acts 1:11**
"...This *same* Jesus, who was taken up from you into heaven, will so come in like manner as you saw Him go into heaven."

**Hebrews 9:28**
...so Christ was offered once to bear the sins of many. To those who eagerly wait for Him He will appear a second time, apart from sin, for salvation.

speculation have brought disrepute upon a sacred truth of Scripture.

The believer's conviction about the Lord's coming should not generate strife but rather a stirring toward holiness (1 John 3:3; 2 Peter 3:11; Titus 2:12–13). Sadly, many believers have ignored these clear passages and have generated disruption within the body of Christ at a local and universal level.

## Affirmations about Christ's second coming

There are numerous affirmations of the return of Christ throughout the Scriptures and we can see that:

1) The coming of Jesus Christ was clearly predicted by Christ himself (Matthew 24:30; 25:19,31; 26:64; John 14:3).

2) The coming of Jesus Christ will be visible (Acts 1:11; 1 John 3:2; Revelation 1:7; Matthew 24:30). Further passages which also speak of the visibility of Christ's return include Matthew 26:64, Mark 13:26; Luke 21:27; Acts 1:11; Colossians 3:4; Titus 2:13 and Hebrews 9:28.

3) The coming of Jesus Christ will be unexpected and sudden (Matthew 24:44; 2 Peter 3:10). Many of the parables that Jesus spoke urge a vigilant watching and readiness for the Lord's return. In these stories, Jesus notes individuals being taken by surprise who have not been properly prepared.

4) The coming of Jesus Christ a second time is not to deal with sin, since his one sacrifice upon the cross was sufficient (Hebrews 9:28).

His first coming was in humility. His second advent will be in great power and glory. This second coming will be accompanied by angels (2 Thessalonians 1:7) and by the saints of God (1 Thessalonians 3:13).

5) The coming of Jesus Christ should be early anticipated by those who believe in him (1 Corinthians 1:7; Philippians 3:20; Hebrews 9:28).

6) The reality of the coming of Jesus Christ and its surrounding truths provide comfort and encouragement to believers during this present age. In 1 Thessalonians 4:13–18, the Apostle Paul after outlining a portion of the events to come urges the believers in Thessalonica to "comfort one another with these words."

### Significant terms

There are three significant terms which are used in reference to the Lord's return:

1) Unveiling—this term points to a removing or an uncovering of that which is now blocking our clear vision of Christ (2 Thessalonians 1:7; 1 Peter 1:7,13).

2) Appearance—this term refers to the coming of Christ out of a hidden background yet accompanied by great blessing and reward. It is literally "a shining forth" (2 Thessalonians 2:8; Titus 2:13).

3) Presence—this term indicates a coming that results in the real presence of Christ being visible from that time forward (1 Corinthians 15:23; James 5:7–8; 1 John 2:28).

**Titus 2:13**
...looking for the blessed hope and glorious appearing of our great God and Savior Jesus Christ...

**James 5:7–8**
Therefore be patient, brethren, until the coming of the Lord. See how the farmer waits for the precious fruit of the earth, waiting patiently for it until it receives the early and latter rain. You also be patient. Establish your hearts, for the coming of the Lord is at hand.

## A general resurrection

The Scriptures also indicate a general resurrection of both unbelievers and believers at the same time:

- Matthew 13:24–30: in this parable, at the time of harvest, the tares are gathered first followed by the ingathering of wheat.
- Matthew 25:31–46: in this further teaching on his coming, Jesus indicates that all the nations will be gathered before him, and he will separate them one from another on that occasion.
- John 5:28–29: all in the grave hear the voice of the Son of Man and come forth, some to a resurrection of life and others to that of condemnation.

## A general judgment

Early church leaders did not speculate much about the nature of the final judgment. Christ himself will be the Judge before whom all will stand.

Acts 17:31
"because He has appointed a day on which He will judge the world in righteousness by the Man whom He has ordained. He has given assurance of this to all by raising Him from the dead."

- The Scriptures clearly ascribe the work of judgment to Jesus Christ (Matthew 25:31–32; John 5:27; Acts 17:31; 2 Timothy 4:1).
- The Scriptures indicate who will be judged:
  1) angels and demons (Matthew 8:29; 1 Corinthians 6:3; 2 Peter 2:4; Jude 6)
  2) every individual of the human race (Ecclesiastes 12:14; Matthew 12:36–37; Romans 14:20–23; Revelation 20:12)
- The Scriptures refer to the scope of the judgment (Matthew 12:36 indicates "every idle

word"; Romans 2:16 "the secrets of men").

- The Scriptures say that the time of the judgment will be at the end of this present age and will immediately follow the resurrection of the dead (Matthew 13:40–43; John 5:28–29; 2 Peter 3:7; Matthew 25:19–46).

- The Scriptures indicate that the standard of judgment is such that saints and sinners alike will be judged by the revealed will of God. Some have had additional privileges which increases their liability to judgment (Matthew 11:21–24; Romans 2:12–16).

**John 5:28–29**
"Do not marvel at this; for the hour is coming in which all who are in the graves will hear His voice and come forth—those who have done good, to the resurrection of life, and those who have done evil, to the resurrection of condemnation."

I desire to have both heaven and hell ever in my eye, while I stand on this isthmus of life, between two boundless oceans.

*John Wesley (1703–1791)*

## 17 Heaven and hell
Carl Muller

Despite all the usual distinctions we make between people (national, ethnic, educational and so on), there are, ultimately, only two types of people in the world. These two groups have distinct beliefs and distinct and separate destinies. Those who believe what the Bible says about Jesus Christ and entrust themselves to his love and saving grace are destined for heaven. Those who do not are destined for hell. Every human being will spend eternity in one of those two places. Hence the wisdom of Wesley's desire! We turn now to consider those two destinies.

**Heaven**
In the Scriptures the word "heaven" can refer to three things:

1) It is used of the expanse above the earth (Genesis 1:8). The splendour of the stars declare the glory of God (Psalm 19:1). These are the "heavens."
2) It is used as a substitute for the name of God (Luke 15:18,21; John 3:27). The "kingdom of God" and the "kingdom of heaven" are used interchangeably (Matthew 4:17; Mark 1:15). The reverence for God that led the Jews to use the word "heaven" in that

**Matthew 4:17**
From that time Jesus began to preach and to say, "Repent, for the kingdom of heaven is at hand."

way is admirable.

3) It is used of the dwelling place of God (Genesis 28:17; Colossians 4:1; Ephesians 6:9). The Christian belongs to God and will dwell with God (1 Thessalonians 4:17), and so heaven will be his eternal dwelling place as well (Philippians 3:20).

We shall focus on "heaven" as it is used in this third sense.

### Where is heaven?

Heaven is a place, the location of which we do not know. We do know that the presence of God is manifested there in a special way (Isaiah 66:1; Matthew 6:9) and that the glorified, bodily presence of Jesus is there (Acts 1:11). In some sublime sense, this heaven, along with the earth, will be renewed, and the believer will forever enjoy the new heaven and the new earth where righteousness dwells (2 Peter 3:11–13; Revelation 21:1).

### Who will be in heaven?

God and the elect angels are in heaven now (Matthew 16:17; 18:10) along with believers who have died (2 Corinthians 5:8; Hebrews 12:23), but after the final judgment all believers, body and soul, who have been washed in the blood of the Lamb, will enter into that blessed existence prepared for them from before the foundation of the world (Matthew 25:34). All of the elect of God will be with God in heaven—not one will be lost (John 6:37,39).

## What will heaven be like?

Difficult as it is to imagine while living in a fallen world, heaven will be perfect (2 Peter 3:13), glorious (Revelation 22:5) and eternal (Revelation 22:5; 1 Thessalonians 4:17).

## What will we be like?

The believers will be free in every glorious sense (Romans 8:21). They will be free to enjoy, unhindered by sin, the presence and the fellowship of God himself (2 Corinthians 5:8; Revelation 21:3). They will be free from the presence of sin (1 John 3:2) and from the consequences of sin—there will be no sorrow, fatigue, death, mourning, parting, failure, fear, need, physical infirmity (Revelation 21:4; 22:2; Philippians 3:20,21). Sorrow and sighing will indeed "flee away" (Isaiah 35:10)! Believers will be glorified (Romans 8:29–30) and finally conformed to the image of Jesus (1 John 3:2). Body and soul, they will be perfect! Whereas there will be continuity (we will recognize each other) there will also be a blessed discontinuity (we will be perfect).

> **1 John 3:2**
> Beloved, now we are children of God; and it has not yet been revealed what we shall be, but we know that when He is revealed, we shall be like Him, for we shall see Him as He is.

## How should we respond to these truths?

The implications of these truths for the Christian are profound. Contemplation of the glory that awaits the child of God will mean

- comfort in affliction (1 Thessalonians 4:18; 2 Corinthians 4:16–17)
- a stimulus to holiness (1 John 3:2; 2 Peter 3:11)

> **2 Corinthians 4:16–17**
> Therefore we do not lose heart. Even though our outward man is perishing, yet the inward *man* is being renewed day by day. For our light affliction, which is but for a moment, is working for us a far more exceeding and eternal weight of glory...

**2 Timothy 4:8**
Finally, there is laid up
for me the crown of
righteousness, which
the Lord, the righteous
Judge, will give to me
on that Day, and not to
me only but also to all
who have loved His
appearing.

- evangelistic zeal (Romans 9:1–3)
- an unquenchable desire to possess what lies ahead and see the One who prepares a place for us (2 Timothy 4:8; Revelation 22:20)

It is an extraordinary fact that Jesus longs to have his people with him in heaven (John 17:24). It is, perhaps, as extraordinary, that our desire to be with him is not as real, consistent and intense!

## Hell

The Bible does not teach *annihilationism* (the idea that all outside of Christ will be destroyed in the sense that they cease to be), nor does it teach *conditional mortality* (the idea that God has created people so that only those who believe in Christ will have immortality—the rest will simply cease to be). On the contrary, it teaches the sobering doctrine that hell is a place of eternal, conscious punishment of all those who have not put their faith in Jesus Christ. It is noteworthy that teaching about hell is found on the lips of Jesus more than anyone else!

**Matthew 8:11–12**
"And I say to you that
many will come from
east and west, and sit
down with Abraham,
Isaac, and Jacob in the
kingdom of heaven. But
the sons of the king-
dom will be cast out
into outer darkness.
There will be weeping
and gnashing of teeth."

## The reality of hell

Some evangelicals in our day deny the reality (and particularly the eternality) of hell. The awful nature of hell makes this, to some degree, understandable. But the biblical data make the reality of hell irrefutable (Matthew 7:21–23; 8:11–12; 13:30,40–43; 24:51;

25:41,46; 2 Thessalonians 1:6–9; Revelation 19:15).

## The justice of hell

There are those who question whether the concept of eternal, conscious torment is consistent with the justice of God. However, the fact of the immeasurable wickedness of sin against an infinite God, coupled with the reality that unbelievers in hell will continue sinning forever (Revelation 22:11), brings the justice of hell into somewhat clearer focus. Emotionally we might find the concept disturbing, but the justice of hell is clearly taught in Scripture (Romans 2:1–16; 2 Thessalonians 1:3–10). Furthermore, a world where there is no ultimate justice for the multitudes who escape justice in this world is surely unimaginable! Surely, after death, judgment must come (Hebrews 9:27)!

## The awfulness of hell

We see the awfulness of hell in several respects:

- Punishment—suffering in hell is not redemptive. Punishment in hell does not aim at rehabilitation. It is, simply, punishment (Matthew 25:46). Those who die in their sins (John 8:21,24) will be punished for those sins. God will "trouble" them, "take vengeance" on them and "punish" them (2 Thessalonians 1:6–9). The fury of the anger of an infinitely powerful God will be poured out upon every sinner out-

**Matthew 25:46**
"And these will go away into everlasting punishment, but the righteous into eternal life."

side of Jesus Christ.

**Matthew 7:23**
"And then I will declare to them, 'I never knew you; depart from Me, you who practice lawlessness!'"

- Rejection—people in hell will be forever rejected and cut off from the presence of God and from every vestige of his goodness (Matthew 7:23; 8:12; Jude 12–13). Though the lost will be cast out from the presence of God, he will be present in hell in the eternal expression of his furious anger.

**Matthew 13:42**
"and will cast them into the furnace of fire. There will be wailing and gnashing of teeth."

- Suffering—the words of Mark 9:42–48 speak of unspeakable torment. Five times in Matthew Jesus describes those in hell as crying and grinding their teeth in agony (Matthew 8:12; 13:42,50; 22:13; 24:51). The pictures used—worms forever eating flesh, torment that stimulates wailing and screaming, agony so intense it leads to the grinding of teeth, unquenchable fire, terrifying darkness—are pictures that point to the reality of unimaginable suffering. Life (if it can be called that) in hell will be devoid of everything that made this world livable and enjoyable (Revelation 18:20–24). All creature comforts will be gone; all sources of joy will be gone. There will be no music and no laughter—only suffering. The suffering of hell is, perhaps, as inconceivable as the bliss of heaven!

### The eternality of hell

In Matthew 25:46 the Lord Jesus Christ uses the same word to describe the duration of hell as the duration of heaven. They are both "everlasting."

Other texts also clearly teach the eternal

nature of the torments of hell:

- Mark 9:43: unquenchable fire
- Revelation 14:9–11: the smoke of their torment rises forever
- Revelation 19:2–3: the saints rejoice over the justice of God which involves the everlasting punishment of the great harlot
- Mark 9:48: *"their worm does not die and the fire is not quenched"*

If the biblical writers wished to communicate the notion of the everlasting, conscious torment of all outside of Christ, clearer statements than these are hardly conceivable. The infinitely wicked sin of those who are enemies of the infinite God demands infinite punishment.

### The deliverance from hell

Only by believing in Jesus Christ in this world can anyone be delivered from wrath in the next world (1 Thessalonians 1:9–10). Jesus Christ is able to save from the wrath to come for several reasons:

- He bears the *punishment* for sinners (Isaiah 53:5,8,11–12; 1 Peter 2:24).
- He was *rejected* by the Father on the cross when He suffered in the place of sinners. *"My God, My God, why have You forsaken Me?"* was his cry (Matthew 27:46)!
- The cup of *suffering* was lifted to his lips and he drank it to its dregs. "O My Father, if this cup cannot pass away from Me

**1 Thessalonians 1:9–10** For they themselves declare concerning us what manner of entry we had to you, and how you turned to God from idols to serve the living and true God, and to wait for His Son from heaven, whom He raised from the dead, *even* Jesus who delivers us from the wrath to come.

unless I drink it, Your will be done" (Matthew 26:42). On the cross, he "suffered once for sins, the just for the unjust that He might bring us to God" (1 Peter 3:18).

- The *eternal* punishment deserved by his people was the reality behind the mystery of his suffering on the cross. In a brief span of time Christ suffered forever for us—God did not spare his own Son (Romans 8:32).

It is this Jesus, and this Jesus alone, who is able to do poor sinners good!

## The implications of hell

Psalm 103:1–4
Bless the LORD, O my soul; And all that is within me, bless His holy name! Bless the LORD, O my soul, And forget not all His benefits: Who forgives all your iniquities, Who heals all your diseases, Who redeems your life from destruction, Who crowns you with lovingkindness and tender mercies.

The impact that these truths ought to have upon each believer is, at the very least, two-fold. The believer should give praise to God (Romans 8:1; Psalm 103:1–4). Humble and heartfelt adoration should well up in each regenerate heart at the thought of such a deliverance, at such a cost!

The believer should also have a passion for souls (Ezekiel 18:32; Luke 13:34; 15). God delights to see sinners delivered from judgment. His people ought, likewise, to desire the salvation of those upon whom the wrath of God is already being revealed (Romans 1:18–32). Christ weeps over impenitent sinners, and heaven rejoices when they turn. His tears ought to be our tears; their joy ought to be our joy.

Let us have heaven and hell ever in our eyes!

The Bible is God's Word, the revealed counsel of God. It is possible for us to develop a certain kind of familiarity with the Bible so that we fail to appreciate the marvel of God's favour and mercy and wisdom in giving it to us. We need to stop and consider what hopeless darkness, misery and confusion would be ours if we did not possess the Bible. We would be without God and without hope in the world, endlessly stumbling over our own vain imaginings with respect to God, with respect to his will for us and with respect to our own nature, origin and destiny. The Bible is the infallible revelation to us of the truth regarding ourselves. It reveals God's mind and will for us; it declares the way of salvation; it discloses the knowledge that is eternal life. The secrets of God's mind and purpose, secrets which eye hath not seen nor ear heard, have been laid open to us, the things that concern God's glory, and our highest interests against all the issues of life and death, of time and eternity.

*John Murray (1898–1975)*

# 18 The Bible: inspired and inerrant
Kirk Wellum

The Bible is absolutely indispensable to Christianity. But not just any Bible. A Bible that merely records the ancient religious reflections and opinions of prophets and holy men, or a Bible that contains a variety of errors is of little use when it comes to the Christian faith. Christians have always believed that the Bible is a special book because it is the inspired word of God, and as such, it is without errors in all that it affirms and can be counted upon to tell us what we need to know about God and the salvation that is freely available in his Son, Jesus Christ.

## The inspiration of the Scriptures
When Christians speak of the Bible as the inspired word of God they are referring to what can be defined as the *supernatural work of God's Holy Spirit upon the human authors of Scripture such that what they wrote was exactly what God wanted them to write in order to communicate his truth*. This definition takes into account both the sovereign action of God and the free actions of the human authors. Both God and men were involved and yet the final written product is the very word of God in every way. The conviction that the Bible is the inspired word of God is based on

what the Bible says about itself. It is not a theological doctrine that has been arbitrarily imposed upon the Scriptures but something that emerges from the text itself. It is impossible to read the Bible and take seriously what it says regarding its own nature and miss the fact that the Bible presents itself as God's Word:

**2 Timothy 3:16**
All Scripture is given by inspiration of God, and *is* profitable for doctrine, for reproof, for correction, for instruction in righteousness...

- Speaking of the Old Testament Scriptures in 2 Timothy 3:16, the Apostle Paul says that the Scriptures have their origin in God himself, they are his breath, he has breathed them out, they are his special gift to his people.

**2 Peter 1:21**
...for prophecy never came by the will of man, but holy men of God spoke *as they were* moved by the Holy Spirit.

- The Apostle Peter brings together the divine and human elements in 2 Peter 1:21. Peter writes that men were involved, they spoke and wrote, but they did so as they were carried along by the Holy Spirit. The word originated with God and he supernaturally superintended the activity of the human authors so that what was written is precisely what he wanted to say.
- In Romans 3:2 Paul refers to the Old Testament Scriptures as "the oracles [or very words] of God."
- Commenting on Psalm 82:6, Jesus revealed his high view of Scripture when he said: "...and the Scripture cannot be broken" (John 10:35).
- Numerous times God is said to be speaking in the Old Testament Scriptures when in the original context it is a prophet who is speaking. In Isaiah 28:11–12, Isaiah is

speaking yet in 1 Corinthians 14:21 Paul attributes these words to the Lord. In Psalm 95:7–8 it is the Lord who is speaking through David according to Hebrews 4:7.

- In terms of the authority of the New Testament Scriptures, the first Christians regarded apostolic accounts and explanations of the person and ministry of Jesus Christ to be the Word of God (1 Thessalonians 2:13). Paul's words in 1 Corinthians 14:37 indicate that he was very conscious of his God-given authority as an Apostle of the Lord Jesus Christ so much so that what he writes is ultimately the Lord's command.

**1 Corinthians 14:37**
If anyone thinks himself to be a prophet or spiritual, let him acknowledge that the things which I write to you are the commandments of the Lord.

- Peter speaks about the writings of Paul as Scripture in 2 Peter 3:16.

- The words of Jesus are also considered authoritative Scripture. In 1 Corinthians 7:10 Paul refers to a command given by the Lord and in 1 Timothy 5:18 he puts side-by-side Deuteronomy 25:4 and words of Jesus found in Luke 10:7 and he calls them both Scripture.

**1 Timothy 5:18**
For the Scripture says, "You shall not muzzle an ox while it treads out the grain," and, "The laborer is worthy of his wages."

- Because the Scriptures are the Word of God, if we fail to believe and obey what they say, we are failing to respond to God himself. In the Bible there are many examples of people being rebuked for not heeding the message of Scripture (Luke 24:25; 2 Thessalonians 3:14). There are also other examples of people being encouraged to heed the writings of both the Old and New Testaments as God's Word (2 Peter 3:2; Hebrews 1:1–2).

**Luke 24:25**
And He said to them, "O foolish ones, and slow of heart to believe in all that the prophets have spoken!"

**2 Thessalonians 3:14**
"And if anyone does not obey our word in this epistle, note that person and do not keep company with him, that he may be ashamed."

**Luke 1:1–4**
Inasmuch as many have taken in hand to set in order a narrative of those things which have been fulfilled among us, just as those who from the beginning were eyewitnesses and ministers of the word delivered them to us, it seemed good to me also, having had perfect understanding of all things from the very first, to write to you an orderly account, most excellent Theophilus, that you may know the certainty of those things in which you were instructed.

**Hebrews 1:1**
God, who at various times and in various ways spoke in time past to the fathers by the prophets...

The nature of the Scriptures as the inspired Word of God does not imply that God dictated what he wanted written. Sometimes God did tell the writers of Scripture precisely what he wanted them to write (Revelation 2:1,8,12), but other times he worked in different ways as in the case of Luke who carefully researched and then wrote about the life and ministry of Jesus (Luke 1:1–4).

Sometimes God revealed himself in dreams and visions, in historical events, and in personal experiences (Hebrews 1:1). We know from the Bible itself that many different human beings were involved in the writing of the Scriptures for a period of more than one thousand years. But what the Scriptures themselves are concerned to teach us is that whatever the exact process of inspiration, in every case, the biblical writers were carried along by the Holy Spirit, so that what they wrote were the very words of God. This was always true even though they expressed themselves freely and in keeping with their own unique personalities and backgrounds (2 Peter 1:21).

Down through the years, some people have pointed to various characteristics of the Scriptures in an attempt to prove that they are the Word of God. Things like the historical accuracy of the Scriptures, the fulfillment of prophecy, the fact that the biblical documents present an internally consistent message, the power of the Scriptures to change lives, the profundity of thought and the popularity and longevity of the Bible as the number one bestseller of all time, all point to the super-natural nature of the Bible. However, in the final analysis, none of these things proves the inspiration of the Scriptures. Ultimately, Christians are convinced that the Bible is the inspired Word of God as a result of the ministry of the Holy Spirit in their lives. Just as the Apostles were dependent on the Spirit's ministry to lead them into all truth (John 16:13) so we are dependent on the Holy Spirit to open our minds and our hearts to the Word of God (1 Corinthians 2:14–15) and the voice of the Saviour who speaks therein (John 10:27).

## The inerrancy of the Scriptures

The inerrancy of the Scriptures is based on the fact that when all is said and done they are the very words of God. The Bible tells us that the God of the Bible cannot lie or speak falsely (Titus 1:2; Hebrews 6:18). In 2 Samuel 7:28 David praised the sovereign Lord as God whose words are trustworthy. Because God cannot lie and his words are trustworthy, it is inconceivable that the original manuscripts of the Bible, which is his Word, contain any errors whatsoever. This conclusion is consistent with what is said elsewhere about the pristine character of the Scriptures (Psalm 12:6; 119:89,96; Proverbs 30:5–6; Matthew 5:18; 24:35).

Recently various objections have been raised against the inerrancy of the Scriptures. Some claim that the actual phenomena of the Bible do not measure up to the numerous

**1 Corinthians 2:14–15**
But the natural man does not receive the things of the Spirit of God, for they are foolishness to him; nor can he know *them*, because they are spiritually discerned. But he who is spiritual judges all things, yet he himself is *rightly* judged by no one.

**Titus 1:2**
...in hope of eternal life which God, who cannot lie, promised before time began...

**Hebrews 6:18**
...that by two immutable things, in which it *is* impossible for God to lie, we might have strong consolation, who have fled for refuge to lay hold of the hope set before *us.*

**Psalm 12:6**
The words of the LORD *are* pure words, *Like* silver tried in a furnace of earth, Purified seven times.

**Proverbs 30:5–6**
Every word of God *is* pure; He *is* a shield to those who put their trust in Him. Do not add to His words, Lest He rebuke you, and you be found a liar.

**Matthew 5:18**
"For assuredly, I say to you, till heaven and earth pass away, one jot or one tittle will by no means pass from the law till all is fulfilled."

**Matthew 24:35**
"Heaven and earth will pass away, but My words will by no means pass away."

biblical characterizations of the Scriptures as flawless and pure. Lack of scientific precision when it comes to events like the rising and setting of the sun, New Testament quotations of the Old Testament that are less than literal and in some cases seem to interpret the original text in a new way, and poor or colloquial grammar are examples of things that are appealed to as proof that the Bible cannot be regarded as without error.

But all of these criticisms miss the point. Inerrancy does not imply a certain preconceived notion of scientific precision, because the biblical writers make use of everyday language to communicate their message. New Testament writers working under the inspiration of the Spirit are in the best position to explain and apply the message of the Old Testament in light of the unfolding events of redemptive history. And unusual or even poor grammatical modes of expression do not necessarily nullify the truth being conveyed in a given passage. It is crucial that our understanding of inerrancy be framed and defined by what we find in the Bible itself and not imported from outside the Scriptures in an attempt to undermine biblical authority. These objections do not nullify the inerrancy of the Bible.

A popular modification of inerrancy involves restricting it to matters of "faith and practice." According to this view although the Bible may contain some historical and scientific errors it is trustworthy when it comes to religious and theological truths. But the Bible itself does not allow us to pick and choose in this way. 2 Timothy 3:16 says that "all Scripture (not just some Scripture) is God-breathed." It is impossible to separate faith and history. God revealed himself in history and the Christian gospel is rooted in history. If the Bible is wrong about some of the things it affirms, how can it be trusted in anything it affirms? If the Bible is wrong when it comes to its own nature as the pure and flawless word of God, how can we be sure that it is right about the nature of God and salvation?

Equally troubling is the inevitable consequence of making human reason the final standard when it comes to determining what is true, and therefore God's word, and what is false, and therefore merely the fallible word of fallen human beings. In the Scriptures, God warns us about adopting such an arrogant attitude as sinful, dependent human beings. We are not to sit in judgment on God's Word but to bow in obedience to it (Isaiah 66:2). Because the Bible is the Word of God, the obedient and thoughtful Christian is left with no alternative but to believe all that it says about its inspiration and inerrancy, and everything else.

**Isaiah 66:2**
"For all those *things* My hand has made, And all those *things* exist," Says the LORD. "But on this *one* will I look: On *him who is* poor and of a contrite spirit, And who trembles at My word."

### Implications of an inspired and inerrant Bible
The reality of this doctrine means that:

- Our Christian faith rests on a sure foundation.
- We can know the God who made us and

has provided salvation in his Son.

- We can know what he requires of us now and until Jesus comes again.
- We should treasure and read our Bibles and hide God's Word away in our hearts.
- When we study and interpret the Scriptures we should compare Scripture with Scripture—other relevant portions of God's Word best interpret God's Word.
- We must approach this supernatural book with faith and prayer asking God to reveal its wonders and riches to us—Bible study is more than an intellectual process.
- It is legitimate to harmonize the Bible's many different parts and seek to discover what it says as a whole about God and his world.

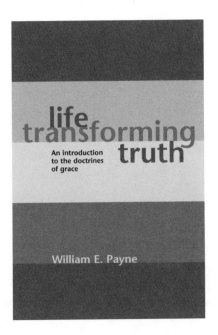

# Life-transforming truth
## An introduction to the doctrines of grace
*by William E. Payne*

Have you ever read the Bible and questioned the love of God? Are you perplexed about how God works in individual lives? Why are some people saved and not others? What does it mean to be a child of God? What does it mean to have faith in Christ? What is the real problem of humanity? Some of the truths of God's Word are difficult to understand. Using simple language and a solid biblical foundation, Pastor Payne answers these profound questions as he explains and amplifies the doctrines of grace. He shows how God works in people's lives to show them their need of salvation, how God saves and how God provides eternal hope for those who trust in Christ. He reveals the glory of salvation and its life-transforming effect on the life of the true Christian. Ideal for personal or group study.

ISBN 1-894400-11-9, 80 pages, 6 x 9", perfectbound, softcover

## Order online at www.joshuapress.com

# Heavenly fire
## The life and ministry of William Grimshaw of Haworth
### *by Esther Bennett*

Though little known today, William Grimshaw was a powerful force in the Evangelical Revival in the north of England in the eighteenth-century. Under his tireless ministry, hundreds in the town of Haworth and the surrounding vicinity came to know Christ. Esther Bennett writes an engaging overview of his life and ministry which will inspire and encourage today's readers in what God can do in the hearts of men and women through his word and the power of his Spirit.

ISBN 1-894400-08-9, 24 pages, 8 x 8″, saddle-stitch, colour, softcover

**Order online at www.joshuapress.com**

# Fierce the conflict
### by Norman H. Cliff

Much is known about the miraculous survival and rapid growth of the church in China in the half century following Liberation, but relatively little is known about the courageous stand that many individual Christians took in the difficult days of the "Accusation Meetings" and the traumatic ten years of the Cultural Revolution.

*Fierce the conflict* relates the hardship and struggle of eight believers whose faith was tested through periods of persecution, imprisonment and forced labour. These carefully documented stories illustrate the sustaining grace of God and will challenge readers to examine their own fidelity to Christ. The author, Dr. Norman Cliff, was born in China to missionary parents and his first-hand knowledge of the country and some of the believers profiled in this volume makes the telling of these stories that much more personal. This book will open your eyes and heart to the work of God in the vast country of China.

ISBN 1-894400-12-7, 208 pages, 6 x 9", perfectbound, softcover

## Order online at www.joshuapress.com

Deo Optimo et Maximo Gloria
*To God, best and greatest, be glory*

Cover and book design by Janice Van Eck
Set in Stone Sans and Stone Serif
Printed in Canada